NAKED

AS NATURE INTENDED

THE EPIC TALE OF A NUDIST PICTURE

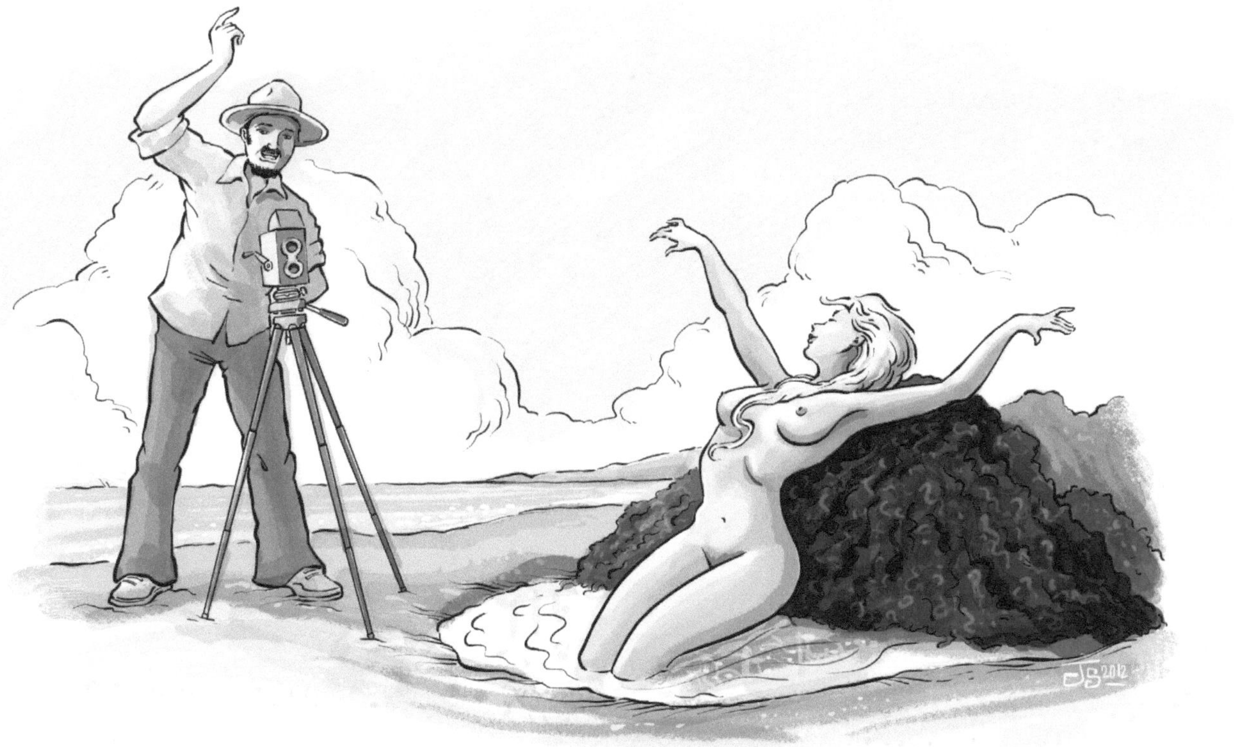

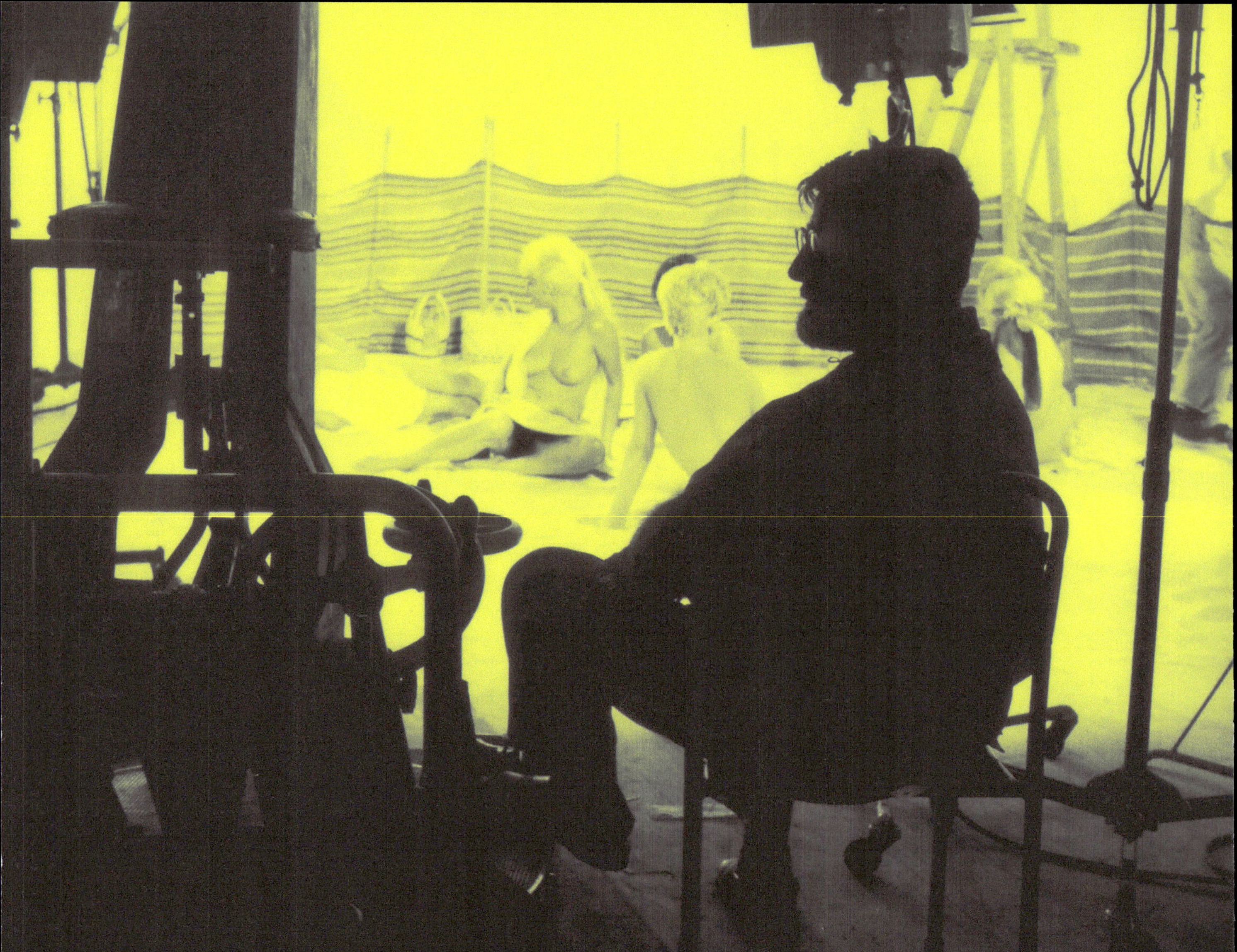

Published by Suffolk & Watt in 2013
www.koreopress.com

Editor: Jay Strongman
Title page illustration by Johnny Stingray

A catalogue record for this book is available from The British Library.

ISBN 978-0-9545985-9-4

Printed and bound by Lightning Source

NAKED
AS NATURE INTENDED

THE EPIC TALE OF A NUDIST PICTURE

Pamela Green

Photography by Douglas Webb, DCM

DRAFT SHOOTING SCRIPT. "C O R N I S

TITLE AND CREDITS

SEQUENCE " A "

A.1. C.U. Typewriter. Office girl. Solicitors office. INT. Day.

C.U. Typewriter showing hands ... working away. Pull back

to show half-shot office gir

A.2. M.L.S. Solicitors office.

Shot shows large area of o

elderly woman at desk cou

A.3. M.S. Second office. Sol

Solicitor seen at desk,

A.4. M.L.S. Solicitors off

Girl puts down phone,

camera screen left.

A.5. M.S. as A.3. Girl

Girl enters and si

---

ots as Sto
eatre, Bed
gnificent coast

ile investi
amela and
Nudist Ca
njoying th
ew friends
ompletely r
he camera c
his new fou
f a typical
any members
........NAKED

BRITISH QUOTA
LENGTH: 5840

SH HOLIDAY.

ion schedule.

4th 7.30.

t 5th

ot 6th

ept 8th

Sept 9th

Septh11th 12th

15th

COMP

CA

PRODUCTION: CORNISH HOLIDAY

UNIT CALL: 7.30 a.m.

ARTISTES
&

PAMELA
PATRINA
JACKIE
BRIDGET
ANGELA

SIDE CLUB

WARDROBE
SHOP SEQU
NG BASKET

TS TOWEL

PASS O
SPORT
MEET

SSING

DAY

ON
NDA

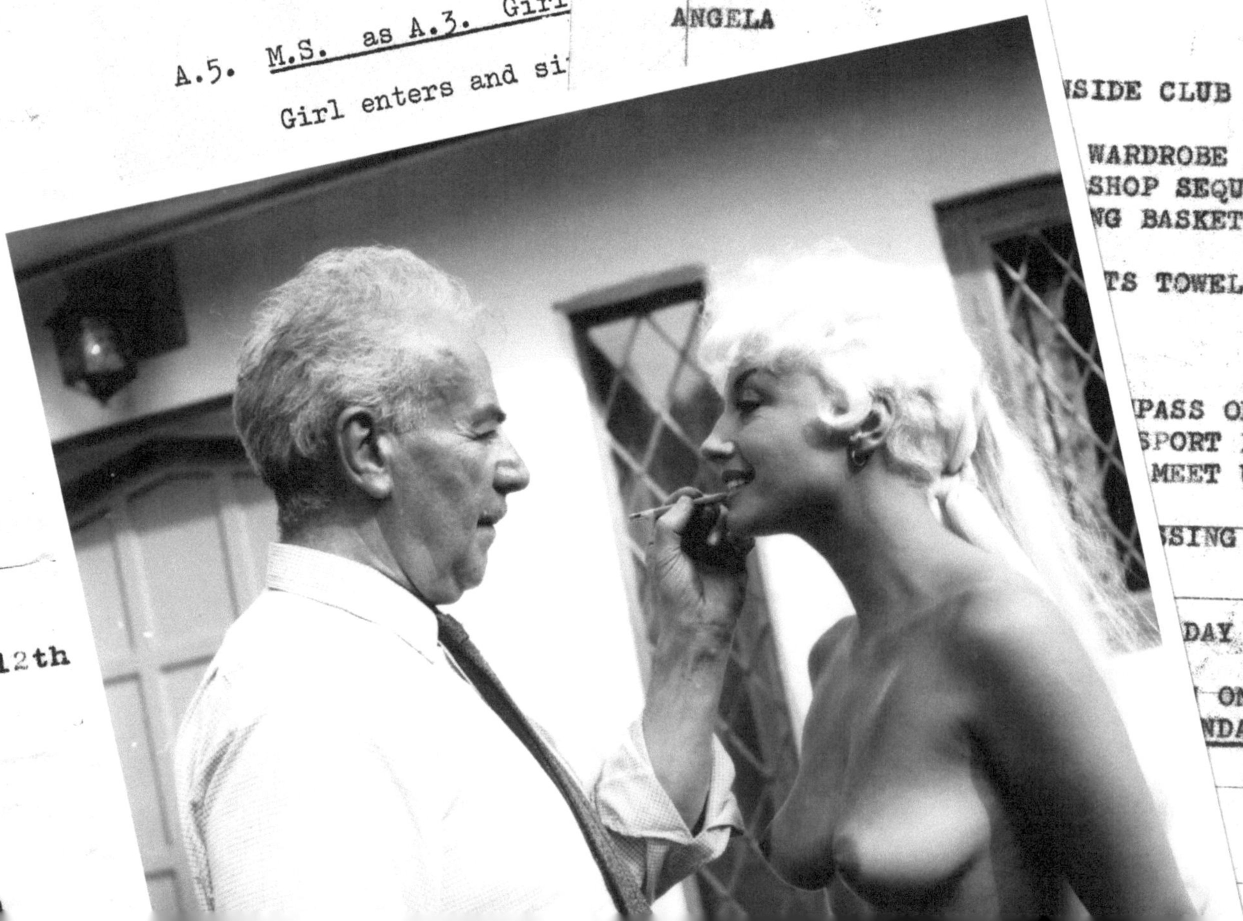

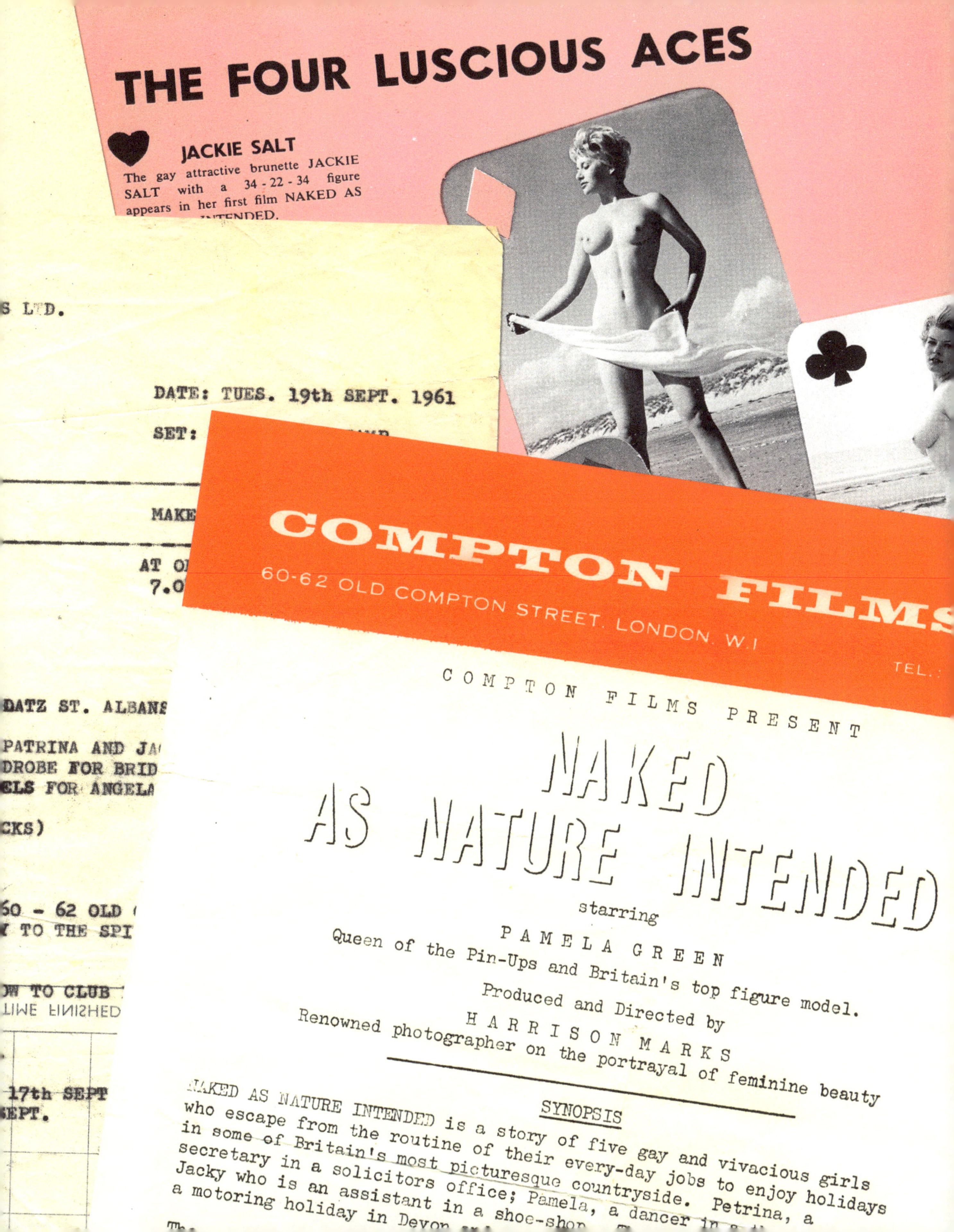
THE FOUR LUSCIOUS ACES
JACKIE SALT
The gay attractive brunette JACKIE SALT with a 34 - 22 - 34 figure appears in her first film NAKED AS
S LTD.
DATE: TUES. 19th SEPT. 1961
SET:
MAKE
AT O
7.0
DATZ ST. ALBANS
PATRINA AND JA
DROBE FOR BRID
ELS FOR ANGELA
CKS)
60 - 62 OLD
TO THE SPI
W TO CLUB
17th SEPT
SEPT.
COMPTON FILMS
60-62 OLD COMPTON STREET. LONDON. W.1
TEL.
COMPTON FILMS PRESENT
NAKED AS NATURE INTENDED
starring
PAMELA GREEN
Queen of the Pin-Ups and Britain's top figure model.
Produced and Directed by
HARRISON MARKS
Renowned photographer on the portrayal of feminine beauty
SYNOPSIS
NAKED AS NATURE INTENDED is a story of five gay and vivacious girls who escape from the routine of their every-day jobs to enjoy holidays in some of Britain's most picturesque countryside. Petrina, a secretary in a solicitors office; Pamela, a dancer in
Jacky who is an assistant in a shoe-shop
a motoring holiday in Devon

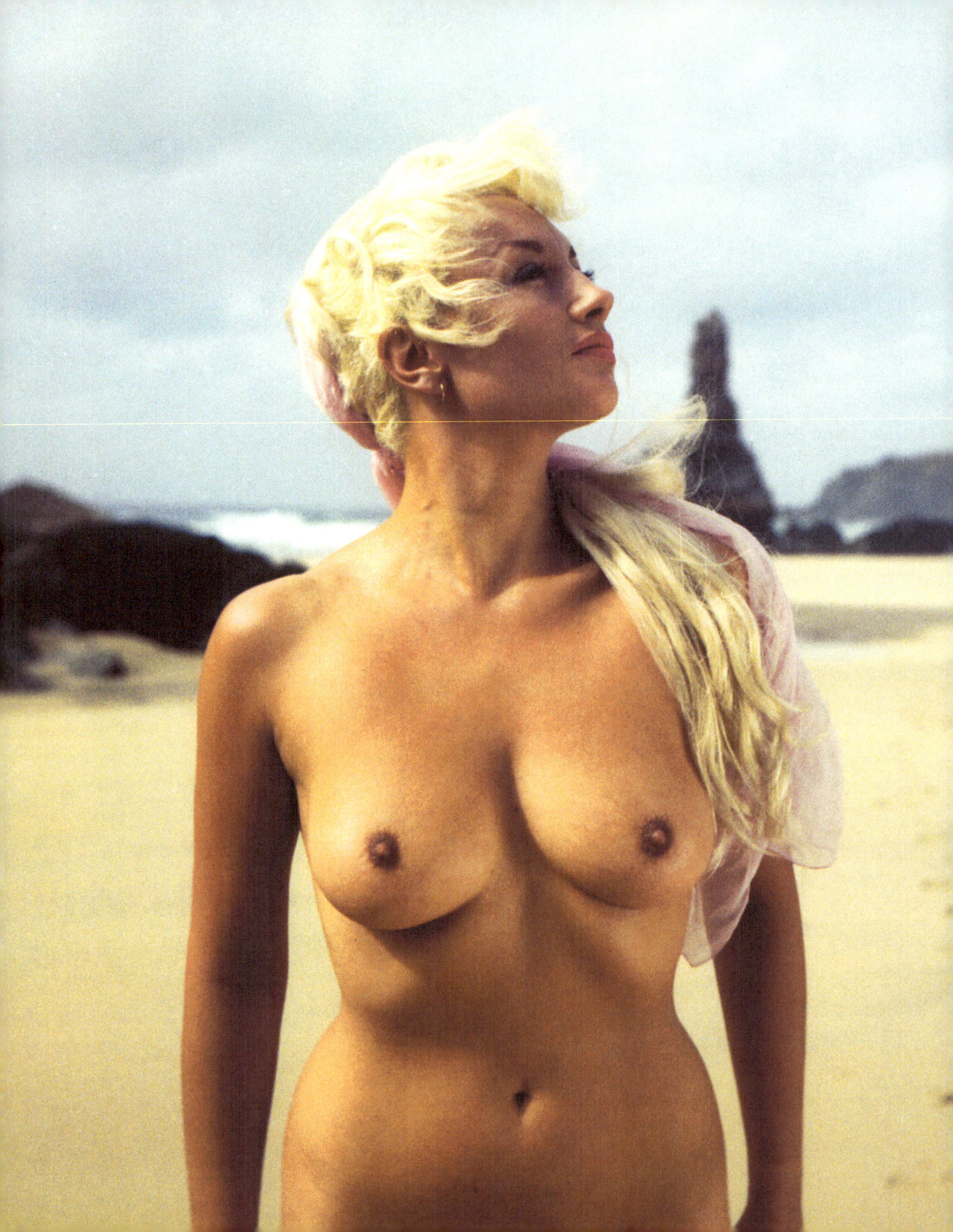

Contents

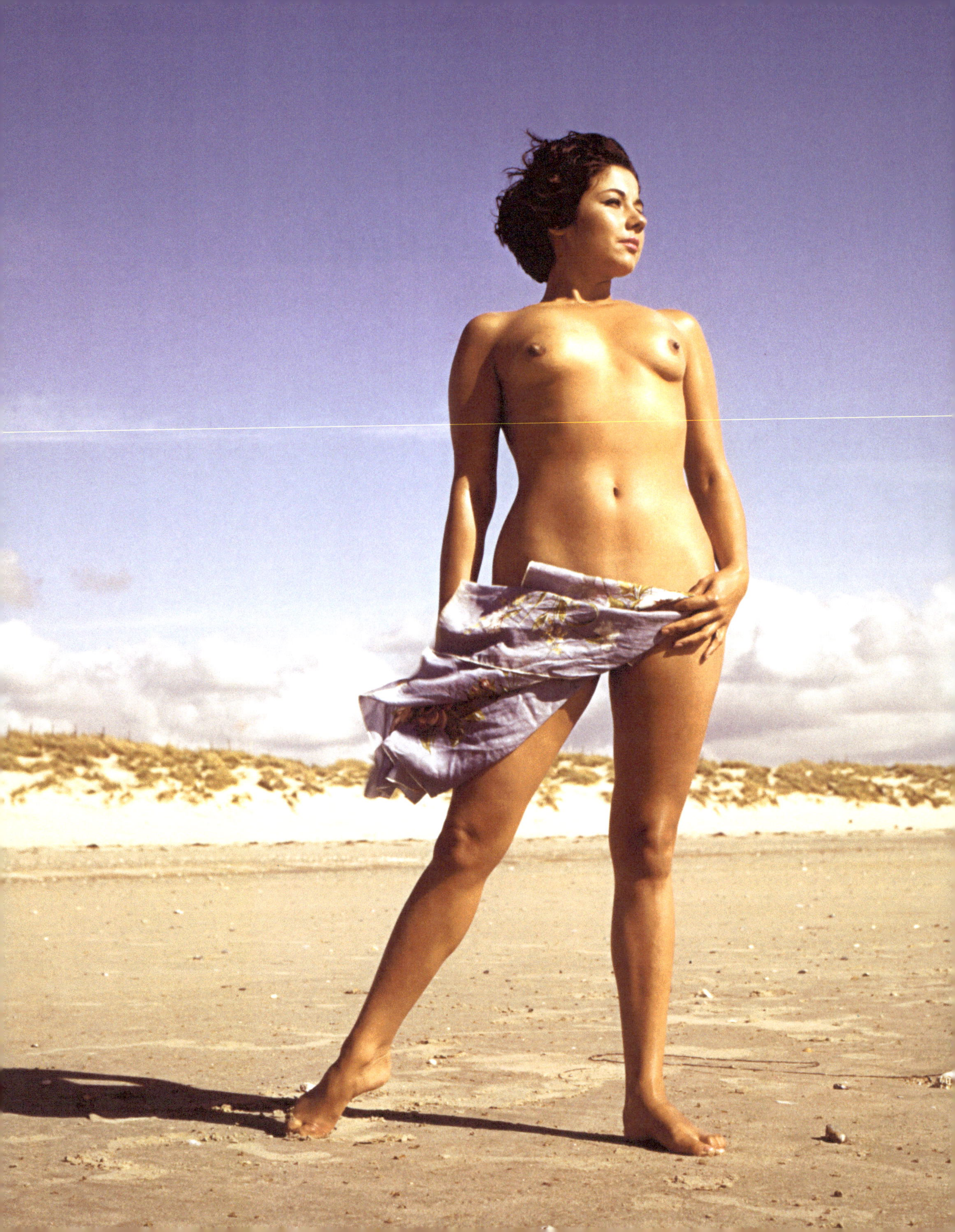

Introduction

I was once told that Jean-Luc Godard said: "Cinema is the history of boys photographing girls." So what better way to start one's movie career than with *Naked – As Nature Intended*. It was the debut feature from Compton-Cameo Films as well as the directorial debut of the notorious George Harrison Marks and my first starring role.

In post-war Britain, the censor would not tolerate nakedness in a mainstream British film. The censors, however, were less strict with continental films. Anything that had to be subtitled was deemed "arty" and of no interest to the general public. Somewhat racier than the domestic competition they proved surprisingly popular, especially compared to foreign films today.

Unable to compete, British exploitation producers were reduced to making 8mm stag films, which were creatively restrictive and financially less rewarding than feature films. Enterprising producers soon realised that films extolling the virtues of naturism would be treated as documentaries — and nakedness in documentaries was acceptable. The first British Nudist film was *Nudist Paradise* (1958). It was quickly followed by *Travelling Light* (1959), *Nudist Memories* (1959), *The Nudist Story* (1960), and *Some Like it Cool* (1961), directed by a young Michael Winner.

It was around this time that Tony Tenser, a former cinema manager who coined the phrase "sex kitten" while promoting Brigitte Bardot movies and an East End Jewish strip club owner called Michael Klinger got together. Klinger ran the Nell Gwynn and the Gargoyle clubs in London's Soho. Their first venture together was a members only cinema club called the Compton. As a member's club, there was no obligation for the films that were shown to carry a BBFC certificate. Their main fare were art house movies from Europe and banned American films, such as *The Wild One* (1953), which eventually got an 'X' certificate in November 1967.

Klinger and Tenser soon realized the real money was made in distributing films throughout the country and not in owning a solitary cinema. They set up Compton Film Distributors to show films uncut in their cinema in Soho and

Left: Petrina Forsyth. According to the film's publicity material the "delightful dark-eyed beauty, Petrina was born in India in 1940. Her mother was a princess, and her father was a British Government official. She was brought up in India until the age of ten, and then sent to England to further her education. She became a nurse in 1956 and was working in Singapore when an Indian film producer spotted her, which led to several parts in various Indian films. Returning to England in 1961, Petrina studied music and was appearing in a concert when Harrison Marks met her. He was struck by her unusual beauty and he suggested she become one of his models. It was natural therefore, when selecting artists for *Naked as Nature Indeed*, that he should offer Petrina one of the parts."
Vital statistics: 34"-23"-34".

then distributed cut versions throughout the country. It proved so successful they struggled to find enough product to meet demand. This motivated them to consider actual film production. There was no way they could compete with the majors, but they could come up with a viable product for their network. As they had a limited budget for studio hire, costumes, and talent, they decided to make a nudist movie on location with a relatively unknown cast. The financial risks would be minimal.

Right: Pamela Green and George Harrison Marks hard at work discussing their photography book *Kamera on Location* (1958).

George and I were acquainted with Michael Klinger. Living and working in Gerrard Street we were just a stones throw away from his cinema club in Compton Street. George had often gone to Klinger's nightclubs taking publicity shots for him, as well as keeping an eye out for good-looking girls to appear in our magazines such as *Kamera* and *Solo*. Besides our publishing company, we had a thriving mail-order business of 8mm striptease films we had produced. Klinger thought George would be perfect to direct and if I could star even better, for I had recently appeared in Michael Powell's controversial film *Peeping Tom*.

George was initially unsure about directing a feature film. It wasn't till Klinger and Tenser took him to dinner followed by a private screening of a couple of typical nudist capers that Marks finally agreed. George found the films so incredibly poor that he vowed "if I couldn't make better (films) than those then I would give the whole racket up". "In that case, you'd better make one," Klinger retorted.

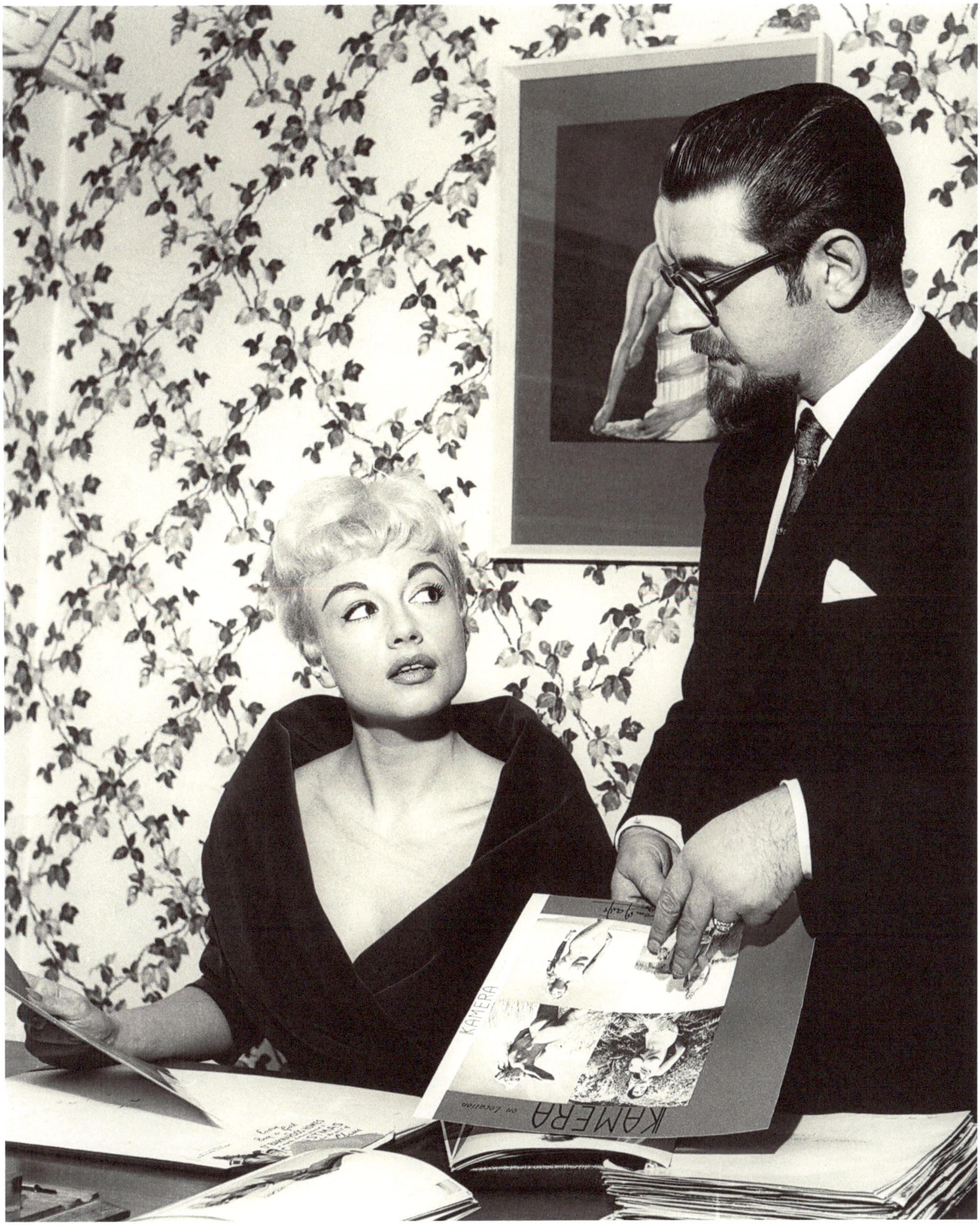
KAMERA
KAMERA
on location

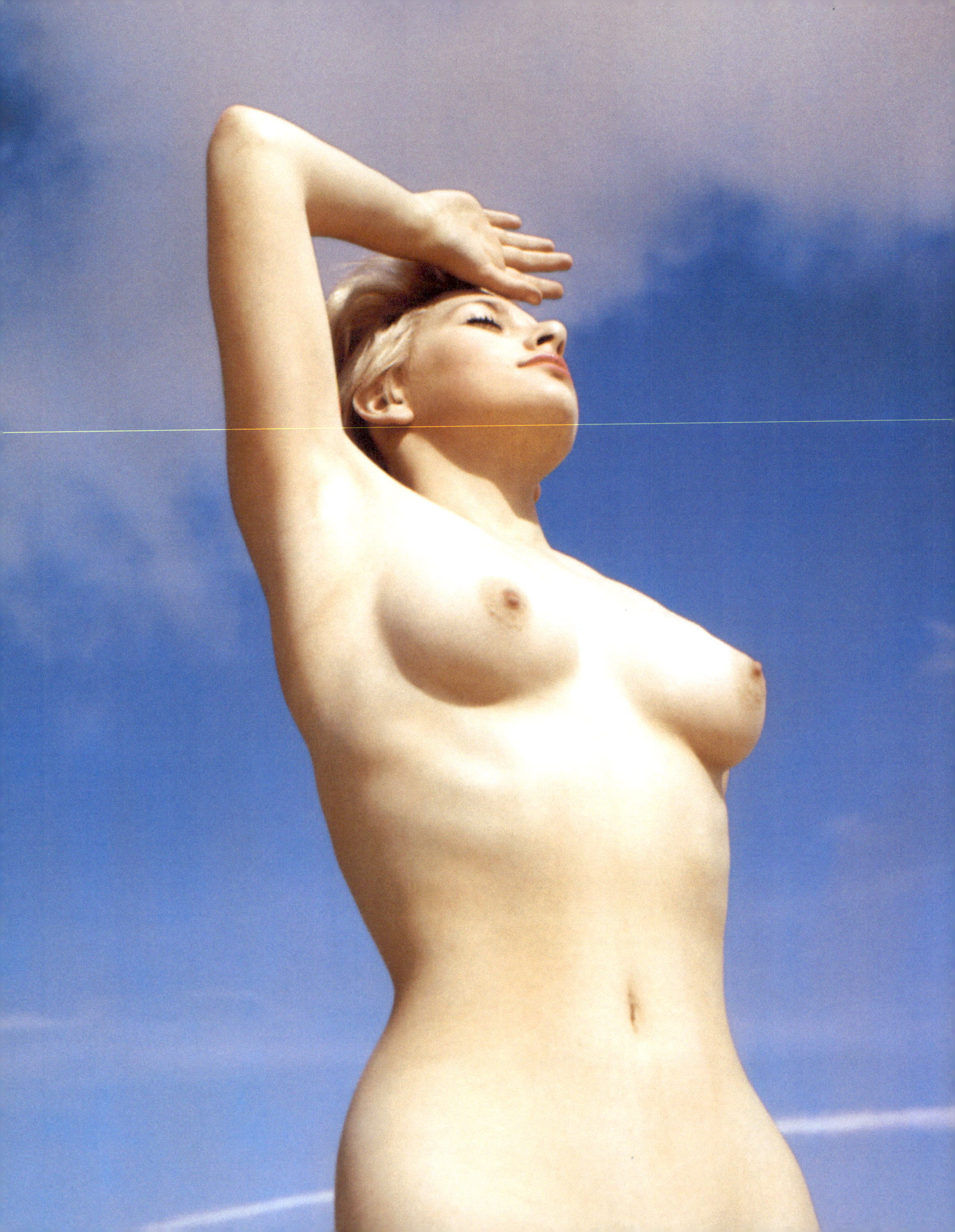

As Nature Intended

The working title of the film was *Cornish Holiday*. Compton Films were to be the Distributors. The Production Company was Compass Films with John Brason as Production Manager. The Lighting Cameraman was Roy Pointer and my good friend Douglas Webb was booked to do the stills photography.

The film was to feature five girls on holiday. I was to play the lead. Four other girls were chosen. Large bosomed girls as favoured by George were out. They had to be modest for they were going to be running about a beach. Large breasts would have been bouncing all over the place. Stuart Samuels, George's friend and sidekick, was cast in a series of cameo roles as a re-occurring in-joke.

Left: Angela Jones. The film's publicity material states that "Angela has a burning ambition to become a top model and with her part in this film it appears that many of her hopes have been realised. Born in Bristol, she and her family moved to Birmingham where a good friend of the family who knew of her hopes thought she would make good progress if the famous Harrison Marks would accept her as a model. On Angela's behalf, this friend wrote to Mr. Marks, and the result was that she was signed-up to appear in *Naked – As Nature Intended*." Vital statistics: 37"-23"-35".

The Synopsis

The story was, to say the least, flimsy. Five girls escape the routine of their everyday jobs and travel down to Cornwall. Three friends – Pam, a dancer in the theatre, Petrina, a secretary in a solicitor's office and Jackie, an assistant in a shoe shop – hire a car for a motoring holiday in Devon and Cornwall. They are not nudists. The other two girls, Bridget and Angela work as garage attendants and they decide on a hiking holiday which will culminate in a stay at a nudist camp in Cornwall, as they are both committed nudists. During the journey their paths cross repeatedly but they don't actually meet till the end.

The film follows the girls through Somerset, Devon and Cornwall, capturing the beauty of the English countryside, taking in such sites as Stonehenge, Tintagel, Clovelly, the Minack Open Air Theatre, Bedruthan Steps and Lands End. While investigating the beaches at Bedruthan, my character unknowingly stumbles onto a private beach belonging to a naturist club, and finds Angela and Bridget, both naked, lying on the sand enjoying the sun and air. I'm shocked but find them friendly. I wave to my two companions to come over and join us. Bridget and Angela soon talk us into appreciating the relaxing freedom of the unadorned body and before you know it we have thrown away our bikinis. We then get a tour of the nudist camp, in this case Spielplatz Sun Club in Bricket Wood, near St. Albans – hardly Cornwall.

Shooting Begins

The Associate Producer and the Art Director had supposedly done a recce of the various locations. Hotels were meant to have been booked and the catering sorted. We were assured everything had been taken care of, so on 4 September, at 7 am, we all met in Old Compton Street, outside the Compton Cinema. Daphne the hairdresser, Gerry, the make-up man, and me plus all our gear piled into Doug Webb's car.

Stonehenge

Top Left: Jackie Salt playing the assistant in a shoe shop. This and the other early scenes of the girls at work established their eagerness for a summer holiday.

Top Right: Bridget Leonard playing an unlikely garage attendant who hikes down to Cornwall to holiday at a nudist colony.

Bottom: Stonehenge, the prehistoric monument located in the English county of Wiltshire, is at the centre of the most dense complex of Neolithic and Bronze Age monuments in England. As a World Heritage Site it was the perfect place for the girls in the film to visit.

The scene – Petrina, Jackie and I arriving by car, George's green Buick, with Petrina at the wheel, she being the only one of us that could drive. We were instructed to get out and walk around the stones. Stuart plays a tourist guide who sells Petrina a brochure. There was much girlish laughter when I attempt to squeeze between the stones.

As the day progressed, it became clear that George was unfamiliar with working with a crew and the 35mm Movie Camera. Fortunately, Roy Pointer was an experienced cinematographer, so we at least had some film to show at the end of the day.

We had no script! There never was a proper script. There was a "rough shooting script", which meant precisely nothing. The first day of shooting was outlined as "Shots of Stonehenge and girls as available". We finished the scene the next day, after which we drove smartly through Somerset and on to Ilfracombe, our second night's stop.

The next day we continued to Woolacombe Beach. It had not been checked out in the recce and it proved totally unsuitable. The day was totally wasted.

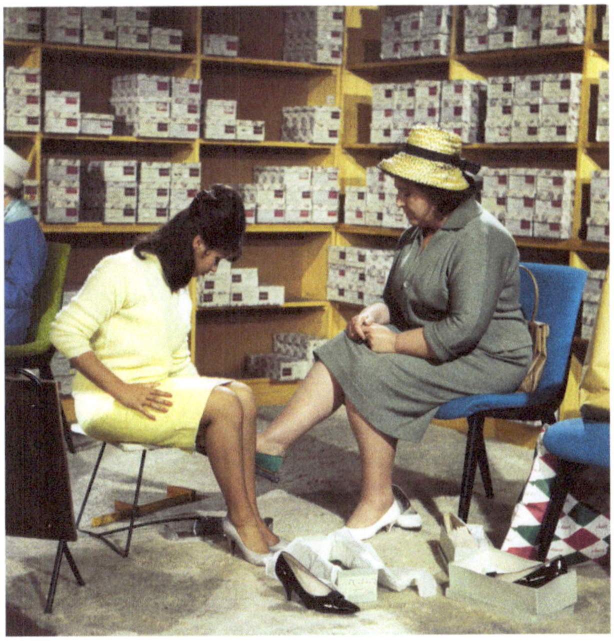

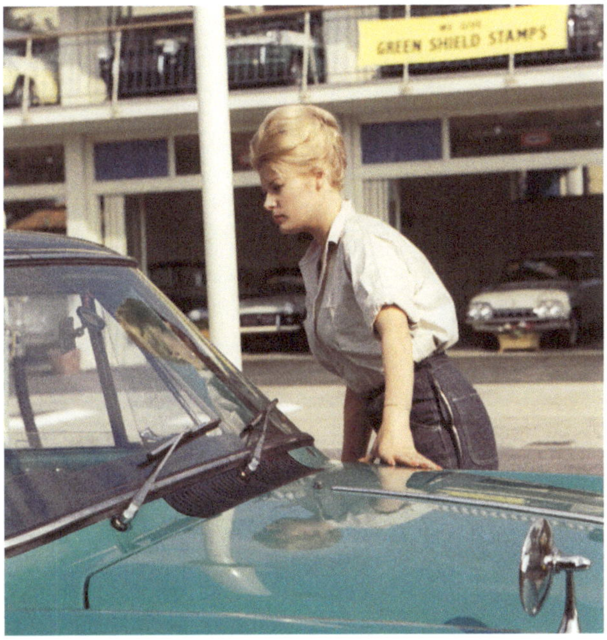
GREEN SHIELD STAMPS

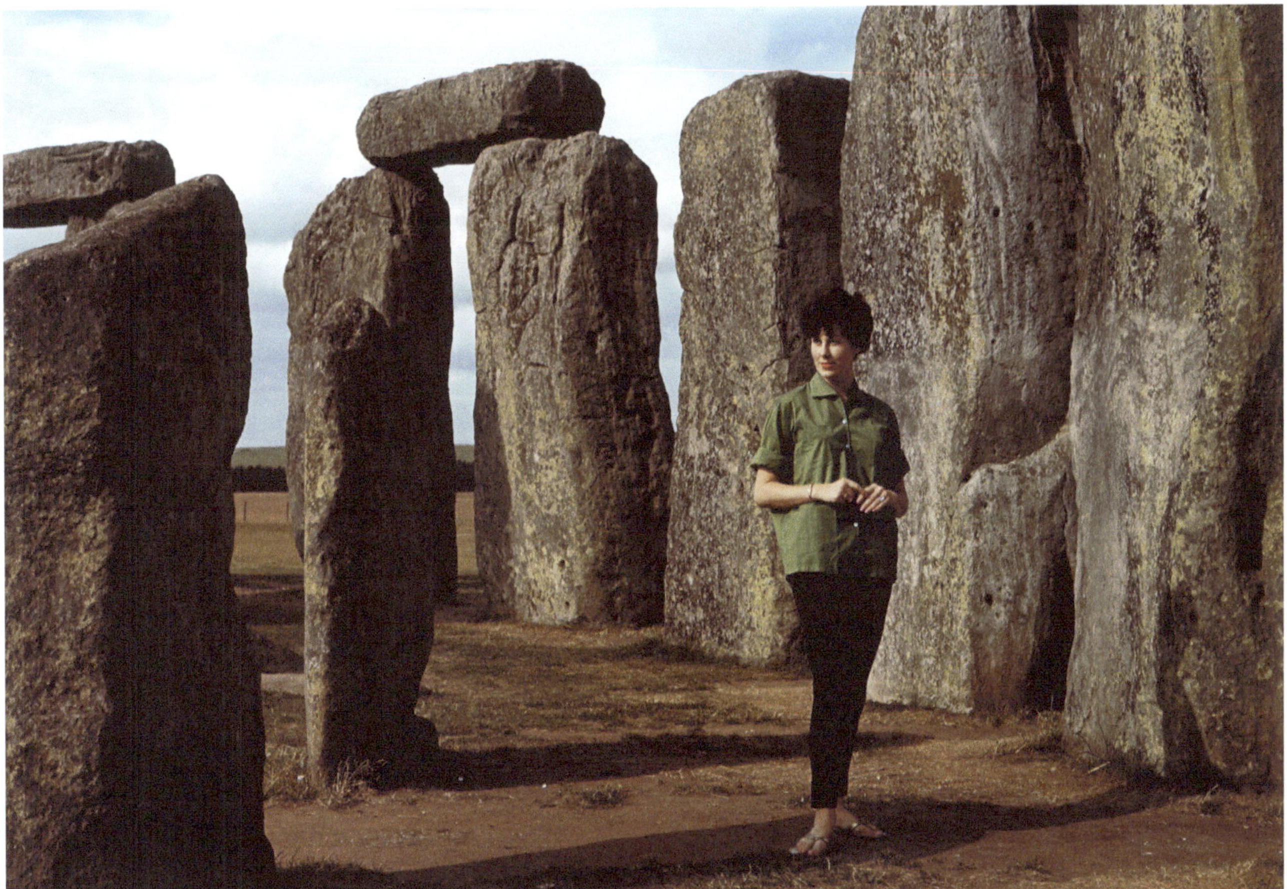

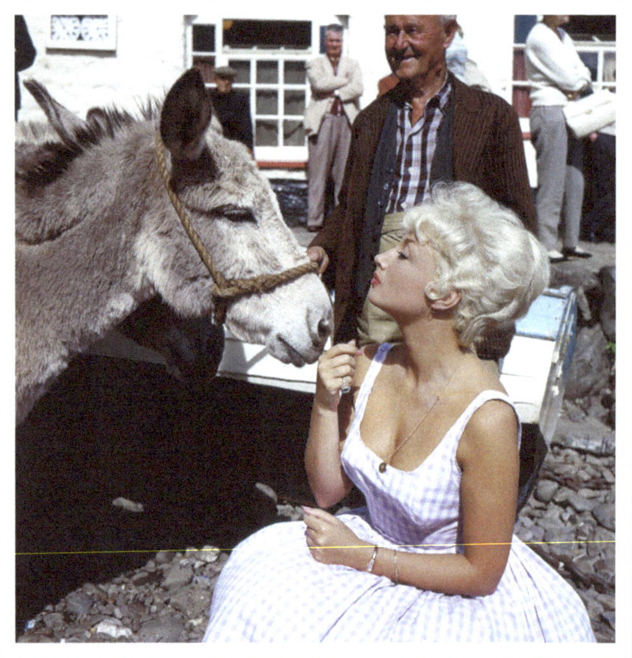

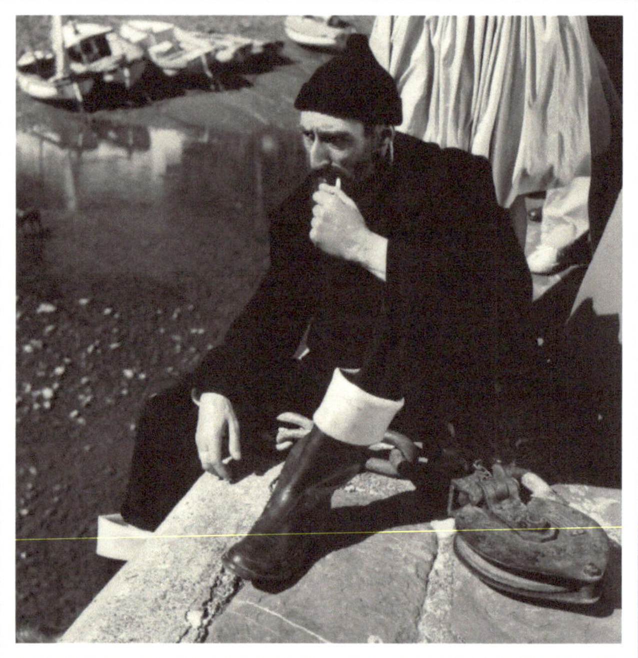

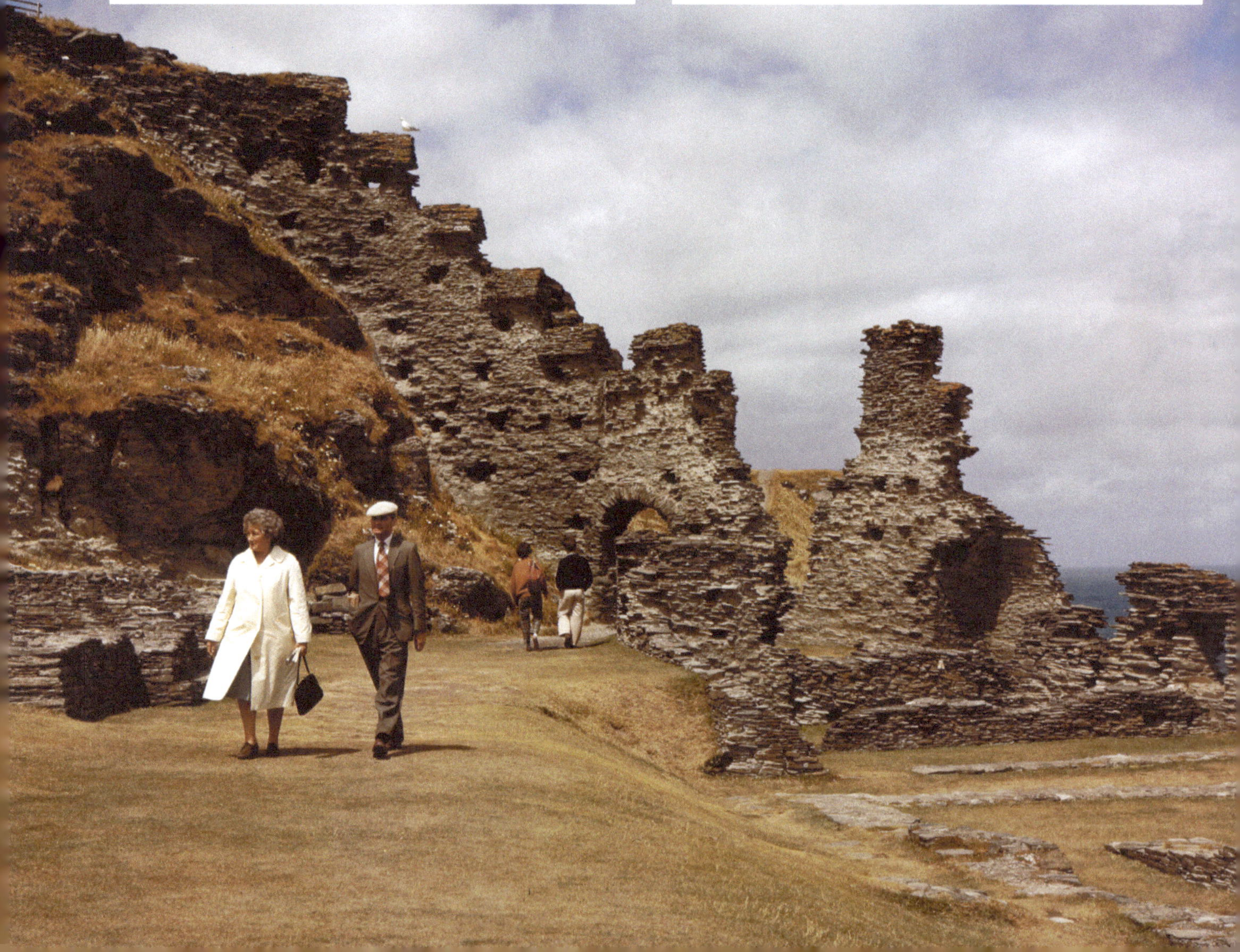

Tapeley Park

Tapeley Park, a Georgian stately home set in magnificent grounds, was only advertised in the Royal Opera Programme. The associate producer and the art director were opera buffs, hence the booking.

We walked through the immense hall and into the main drawing room, both magnificently furnished. A butler brought us tea and cucumber sandwiches on a silver tray. Not the place for a film unit and five nubile girls. At dinner that night, in the resplendent dining room, an elderly gentleman came in and took his place at the head of the table. At precisely 8 pm, he rose and raised his glass to the Queen. Dinner was then served. We were puzzled about this, but Doug twigged it. At 8 pm the curtain goes up at Glyndebourne opera house! The gentleman was none other than John Christie, who founded the Glyndebourne Opera Festival way back in 1934. That night I slept in a magnificent bedroom, spacious enough to accommodate the make-up and hairdressing department as well.

Clovelly and Tintagel Castle

The following day, we were in the ancient village of Clovelly, where Petrina, Jackie and I passed Bridget and Angela in the street. The main thoroughfare, known as Up-along and Down-along, tumbles its cobbled way down 400ft of solid rock to the tiny harbour. The village is famous for its donkeys, which traditionally carry goods up the hill while sledges bring things down. We were to wear our summer dresses. "Ooops! Did I have to bring a frock ?" a round-eyed Petrina asked. Fortunately, I had brought two. George got us to stroke the donkeys and Stuart was to play a fisherman with a clay pipe, leaning against the harbour wall. A couple of passing elderly ladies asked Stuart "Are you a real fisherman?" He told them that he was an actor in costume and make-up. "They didn't half give you a big nose — you look like some old Yid!" one of the ladies blurted out. Stuart, who was Jewish and whose nose was real, burst out laughing.

That afternoon, when we had finished filming, I boarded the train to London. The next scene involved Bridget and Angela only, clumping up and down Tintagel Castle, a place of 'magic casements', opening on the foam of perilous seas. Petrina, Jackie and I had the day off.

Top Left: Pamela Green at the ancient harbour village of Clovelly in North Devon with one of the village's famous donkeys.

Top Right: Stuart Samuels. According to the film's publicity material Stuart "was born in 1927 three doors away from the house in Tottenham where Harrison Marks was born one year earlier. The two have been firm and inseparable friends since they were able to talk. On leaving school at the age of fourteen, Stuart entered the film business, and when Harrison Marks began producing children's short comedy films they appeared together in many of the slapstick sequences. It was a natural choice therefore when Harrison Marks was casting for *Naked – As Nature Intended* to place the comedy material in the hands of his old friend and partner Stuart Samuels."

Bottom: Set high on the rugged North Cornwall coast, Tintagel Castle, offers dramatic views while being steeped in legend and mystery; said to be the birthplace of King Arthur as well as featuring in the tale of *Tristan and Isolde.*

Minack Theatre

It had been arranged that I could have my hair bleached and my switches set the following morning by Eileen, and return on the night train to Penzance for the location at the Minack Theatre, an open-air theatre located right on the coastline of Porthcurno Bay with spectacular views of the Atlantic ocean. "Book your return on the night train that leaves around 11 pm when you arrive at Paddington", I was told. At the booking office I discovered that there were two trains; one a non-sleeper at 11 pm, arriving at Penzance about 8 am and a sleeper which left at midnight and arrived at Penzance half an hour after the other train. I booked the sleeper, as a good night's rest was preferable to sitting up in a carriage all night. Doug rang me that evening at my flat and I explained what I had done. The next night with my hair bleached and the two switches in place ready for the next morning, I boarded the sleeper.

Top: Jackie Salt, Pamela Green and Petrina Forsyth running down the steps at the spectacular Minack Theatre. The blustery conditions gave director Marks a chance to get some candid shots of the girls' bare thighs and knickers as the wind blew their skirts up around their waists.

Bottom Left: George Harrison Marks in his cameo role as a theatre producer, with Pamela Green and Jackie Salt listening attentively.

Bottom Right: Stuart Samuels posing as Hamlet at the Minack Theatre.

A frieze of angry heads looked down at me as I walked down the platform at Penzance. "Where had I been? I was late, why wasn't I on the earlier train?" My hair, I told them, was ready; all I needed was make-up. I also pointed out that I was rested, which I certainly would not have been sitting up in a carriage all night. Somewhat mollified, John Brason gave the order to move off.

At the Minack Theatre at Porthcurno, with its backdrop of clouds and the Atlantic, we stood so that the wind blew our skirts up. George's idea was to get a glimpse of bare thigh and knickers. Stuart dressed in black tights and a blonde wig was instructed to do an "Oliver", while George pretended to be a theatre producer planning a rehearsal.

We climbed yet another set of stairs, high above the camera; more flashes of knickers. I was told to stop and do a 'windswept pose'. With my hair blowing across my face and my skirts billowing around my ears, they saw a lot more than a glimpse of the G-String I was wearing. A frown from Brason. "I don't think that sort of shot would go down well with the Naturist Movement, George."

We then all drove off to Lands End, leaving the camera crew to do some "Pretty (topographical) shots to round off the sequence".

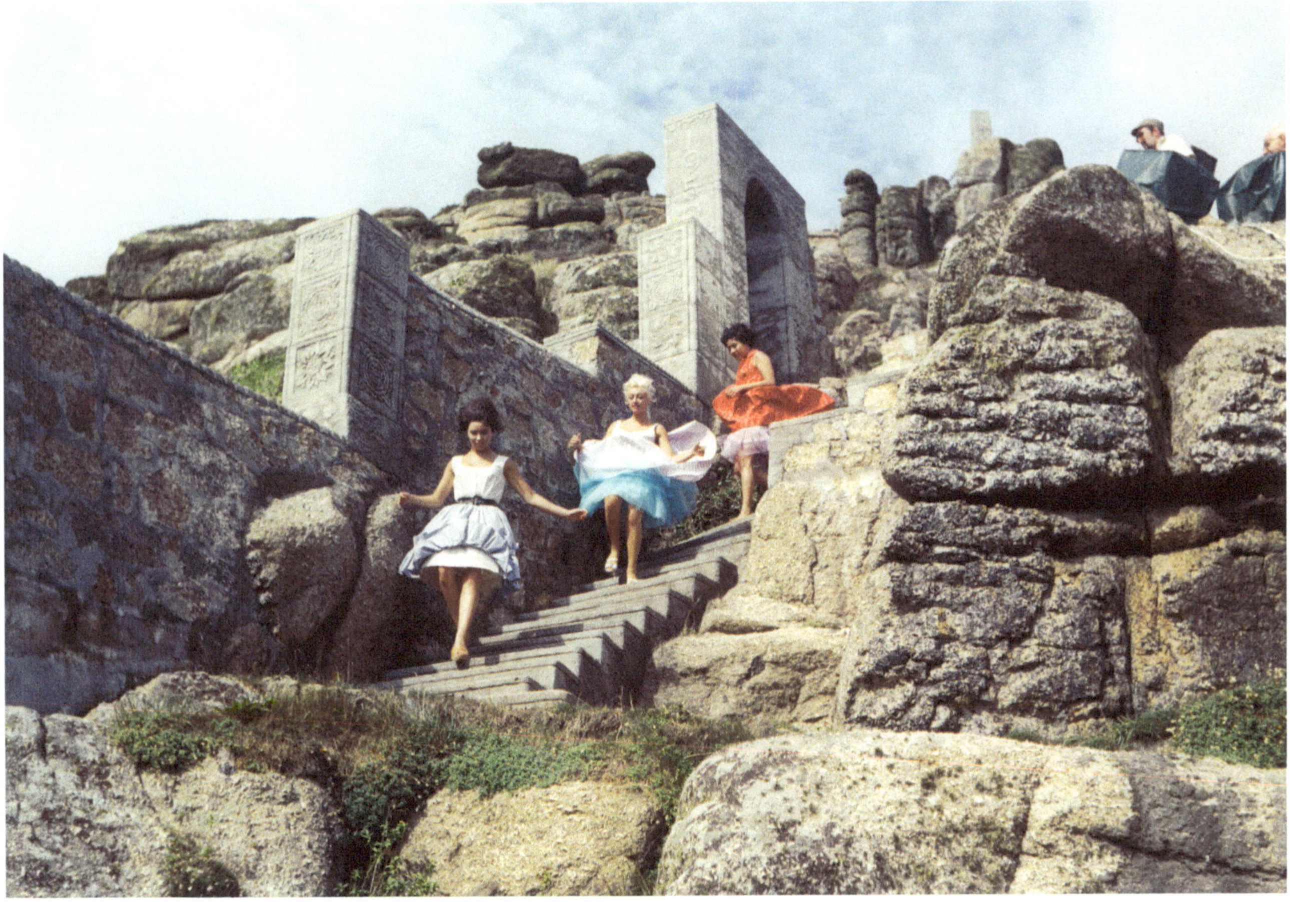

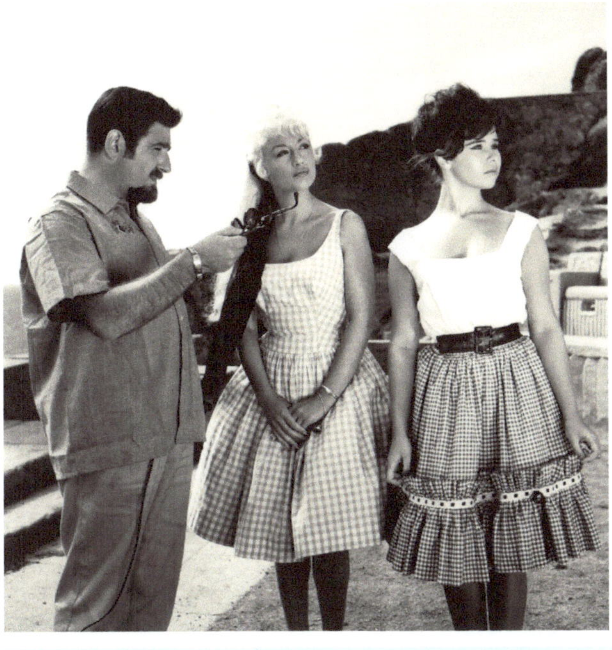

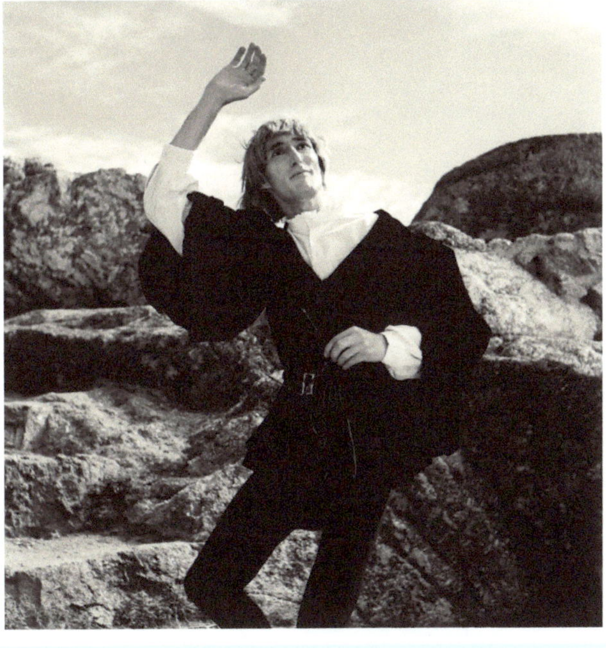

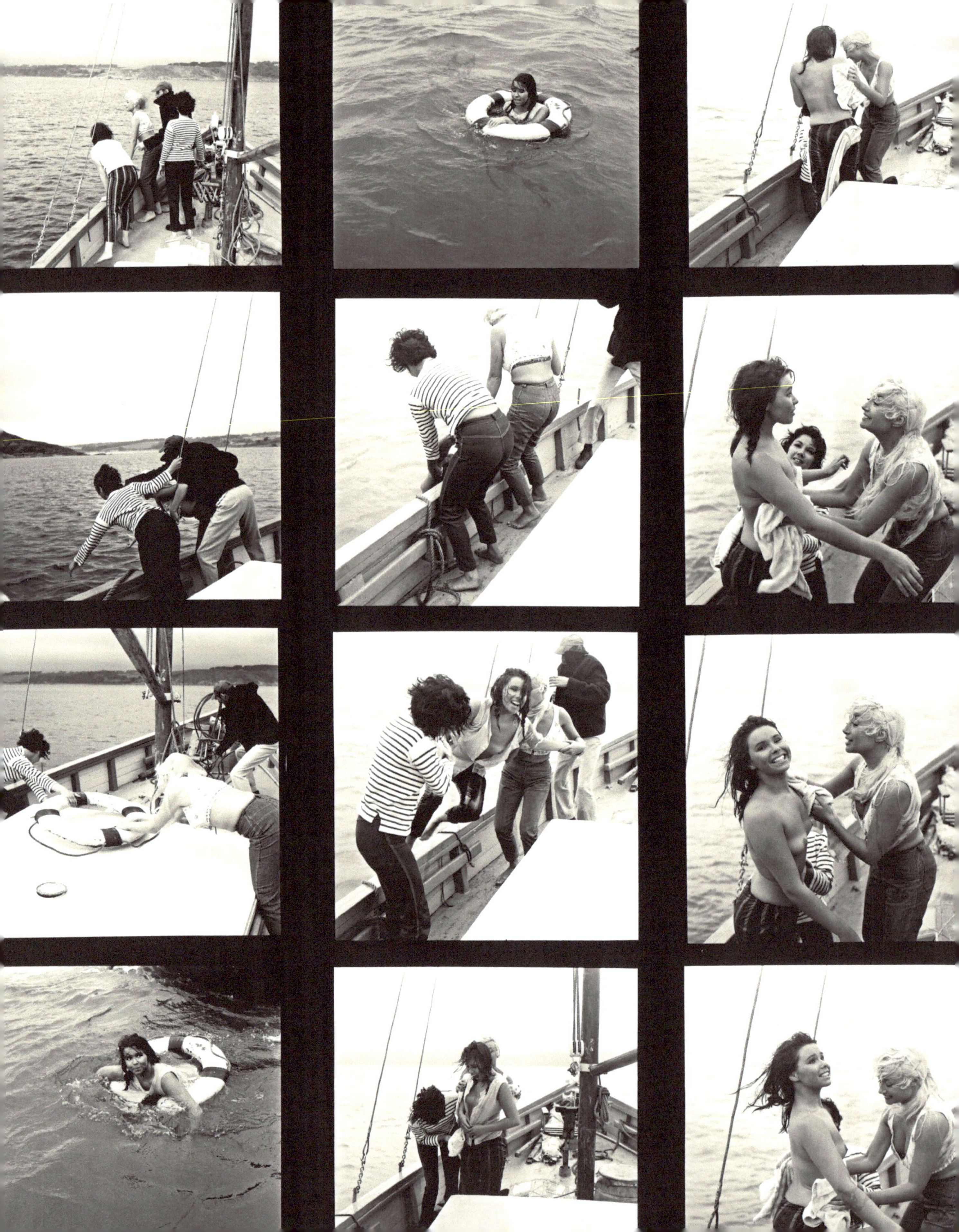

Lands End and out to sea at Falmouth

At Lands End the three of us ran around in shorts clutching ice creams, buying postcards and waving. That night we stayed at Helston. As far as locations specified in the shooting script were concerned, we had lost Exmoor, Hunters Inn at Coombe Martin, Jamaica Inn and Princetown.

George, however, came up with the bright idea that the three of us on a boat might be fun. At Falmouth Brason found a fishing boat for hire – a fair sized craft that took people out shark fishing.

Left: The notorious rubbing down sequence on the fishing boat that was cut from the UK version of the film.

Stuart was to be the fisherman. In the stern it was somewhat cramped with the camera and the crew. George worked out the action with his usual flair. One of us could fall overboard. Jackie volunteered. At the given moment, George told her to fall in, which she did, except that in her enthusiasm, she leapt rather than fell. Stuart the shark fisher dropped his line and came staggering along. I tripped over the main hatch cover, banging my head on the boom. Petrina hopping up and down delivers the line "Ooh, Jackie's fallen in!" It was rather stating the obvious.

Like a drowned puppy, hair all over her face, Jackie was hauled up. "Rub her down! " came the instructions. We all did. By now, Jackie was shaking with cold and we weren't much better. "They won't wear it, George", Brason said. "Women rubbing each other down!" All you see in the UK cut of the film is Jackie standing on the edge of the boat. The next minute she appears unaccountably wet and bedraggled.

Bedruthan Steps

Bedruthan Steps is a truly spectacular landscape on the north Cornish coastline, a few miles east of Newquay. The cliffs at Bedruthan have been systematically eroded over the years, leaving a series of impressive volcanic rock stacks. These pillars of detached cliff rise from Bedruthan Beach, forming a series of columns that stretch across the bay from Pendarves Island to Diggory's Island. Legend has it that a giant called Bedruthan used the rocks stacks as stepping stones. To get to the beach one has to negotiate 100 steep steps down a precipitous cliff face. This was to be the location for the major nude scenes.

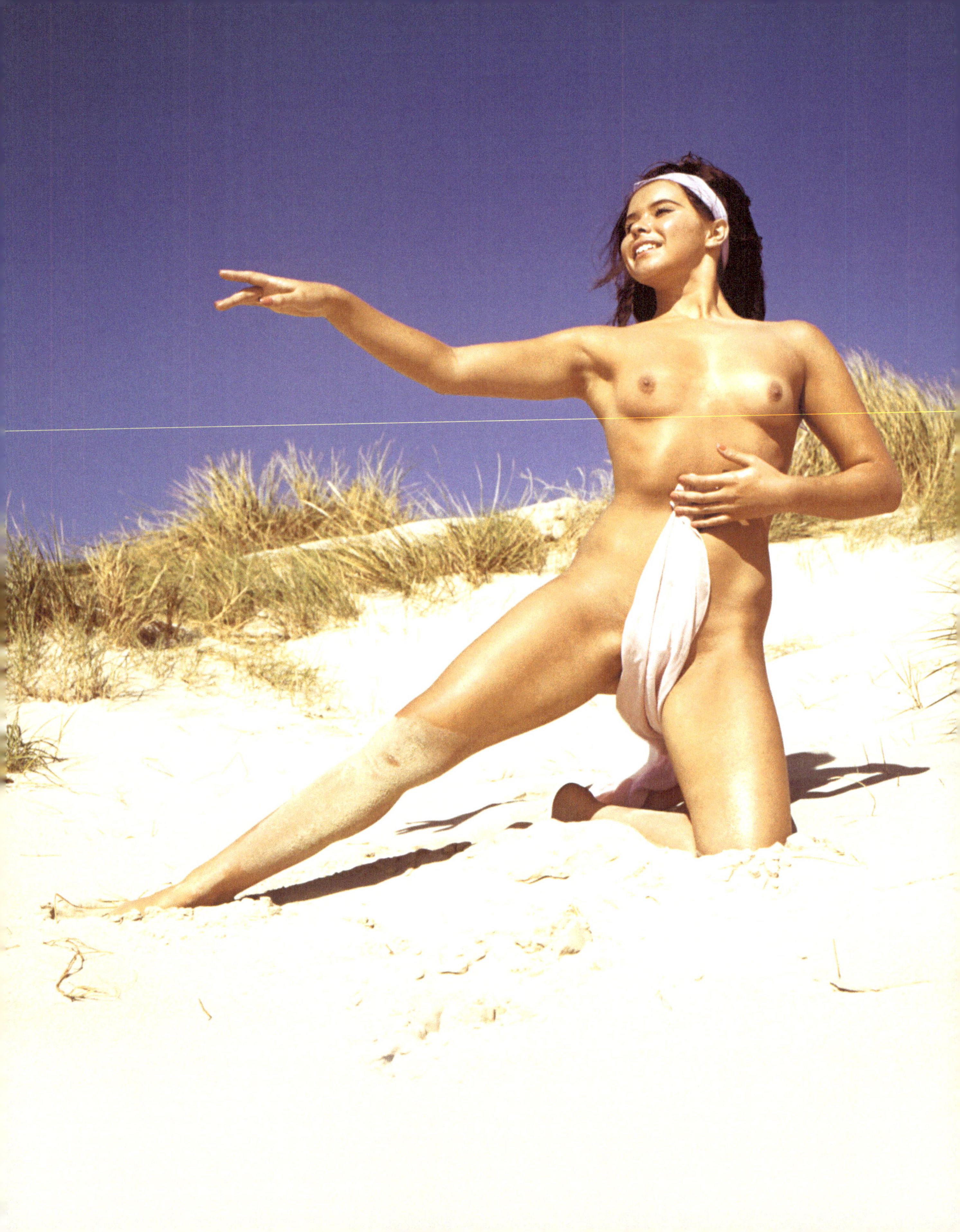

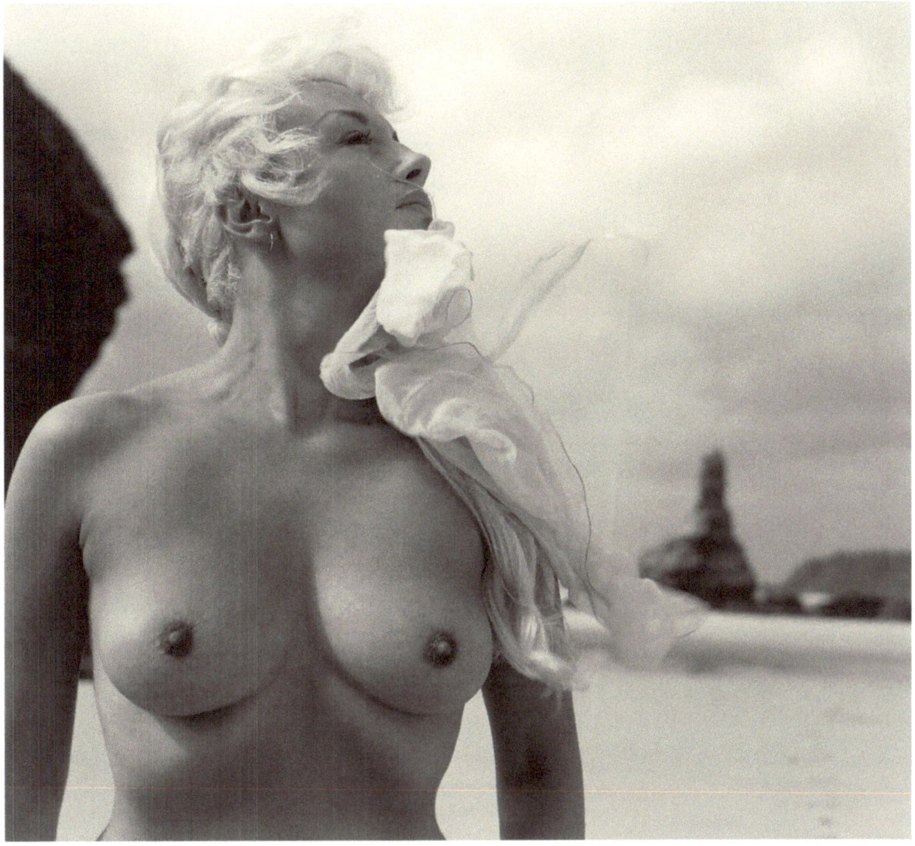

Far Left: Jackie Salt. As the film's publicity material makes known "the gay attractive brunette Jackie appears in her first film *Naked – As Nature Intended.* After leaving school Jackie commenced work as a secretary in a local office, but on learning from a friend that Harrison Marks had a vacancy she attended an interview and thus commenced a successful career as a model. When it came to casting for *Naked – As Nature Intended*, Jackie seemed a natural choice, and as one will see the decision was amply justified. Now studying at drama school, Jackie hopes one day to become an actress."
Vital statistics: 34"-22"-34".

Left: Pamela Green. A shot from the opening title sequence filmed on Bedruthan Beach. A similar image was used on the UK film poster.

The opening title was me walking from the edge of the sea across the beach and into camera. Roy had marked a line in the sand; I was to stop there. In the long shot, there would be no problem showing the pubic area, especially if I could walk in such a way that nothing could be seen to alarm the censors. This I could do by swivelling the hips so that the leg always cut across the offending area. For safety's sake, I was to carry a towel in one hand. Casually placing it across my stomach as I stopped in front of the camera. This was to be in one take. There was no rehearsal, so as not to leave footprints in the sand. I stood in the sea and waited for the signal. From the edge of the surf I walked across the sand towards a small pool George wanted me to walk through. I stepped into it expecting it to be shallow. At the deepest point, it was nearly six feet! I could hardly disappear in the opening shot and somehow I managed to pull myself out. I walked around the camera operator and into camera, stopping on the mark. George came bustling up. "What was all that kerfuffle by the pool?" "Next time," I said, "Measure it!"

George had bought an enormous beach ball and we were told to chase about with considerable spirit. The wind kept catching the wretched thing. All five

Below Left: George Harrison Marks at Bedruthan Steps.

Below Right: Petrina Forsyth with a beach ball waiting for a light meter reading on the chilly beach.

of us were now stripped off. Petrina, standing on a rock, suddenly became coy, covering herself with her hands exclaiming that everyone could see her "Biscuit". Cold and wet, my patience at an end, I told her to take her hands from her blasted "biscuit": and threw her the beach ball, "Catch!". Still muttering "Oooo my biscuit", under her breath, she ran awkwardly with her legs prudishly clamped tight together.

Apart from locations not seen, we were finding hotels not booked or unable to accommodate a unit of some twenty people. At Bedruthan, having cancelled the previous booking at Wadebridge, they put us in an unsuitable hotel full of mums and screaming children. Half the crew found themselves without a room and had to search locally for accommodation. The five of us had to share one smallish room. Extra beds had been moved in and put up dormitory style.

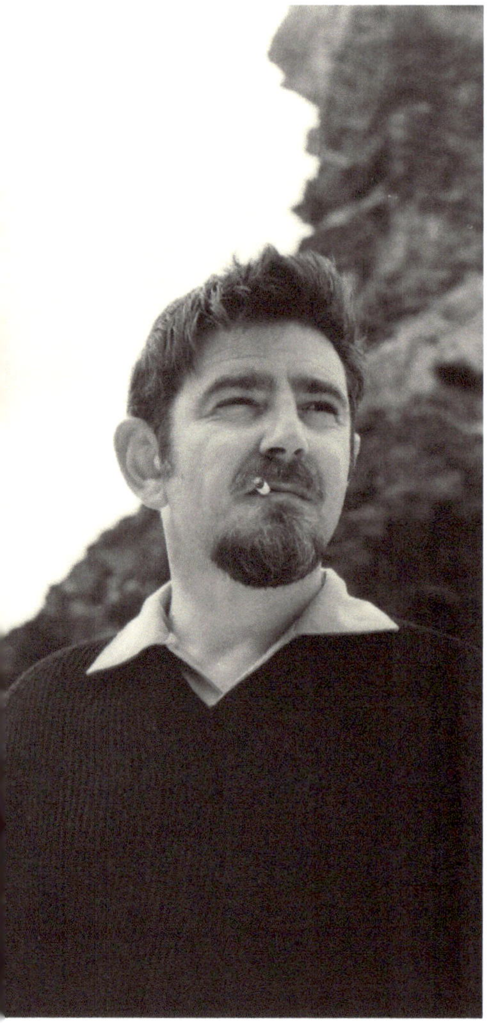

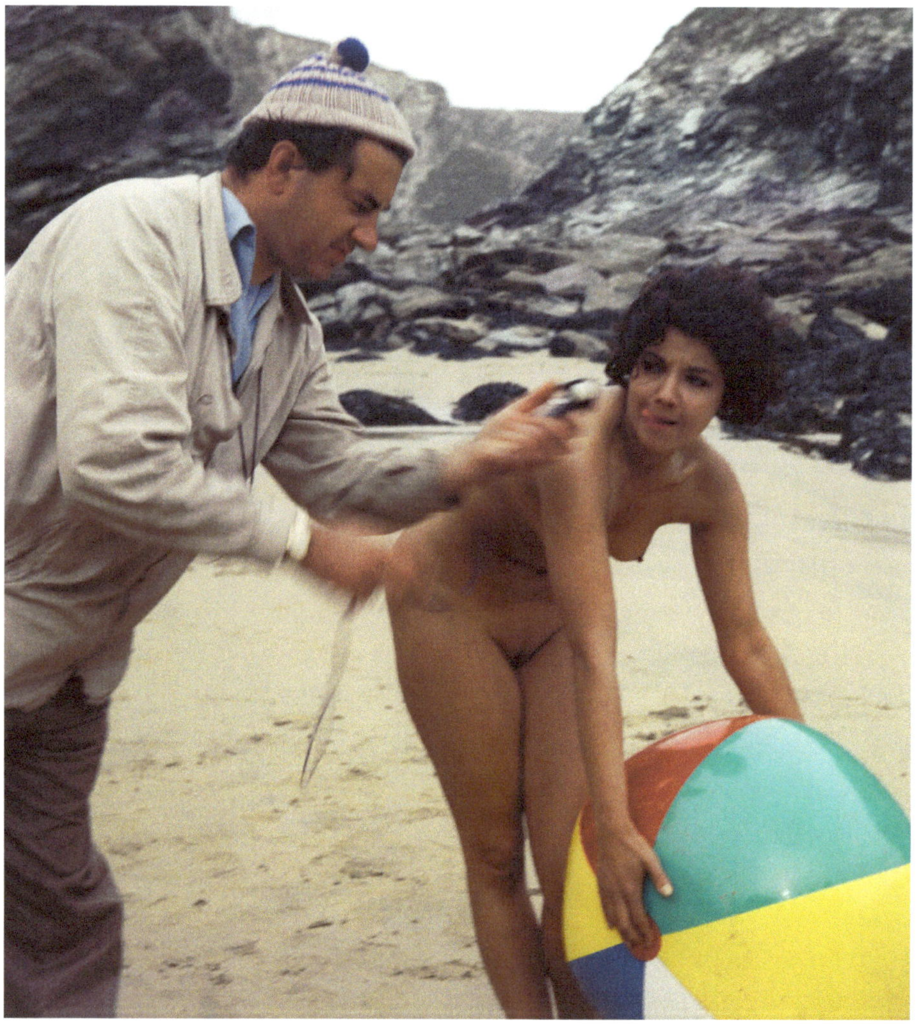

Brason roused us the next morning, army fashion. "Out of bed, all of you, and be quick about it." Standing there in his khaki jacket and cap, he bore a strong resemblance to Castro, which became his nickname for the rest of the film.

At Bedruthan Steps the tide was out when we began the second day's shooting on the beach. This was to be a long sequence of me swimming nude in a rock pool. Roy filmed me while I swam slowly into camera, and around the pool. I had left my towel on the sand between Roy on the camera and the sea. Doug taking pictures noticed that the beach was disappearing and the rocks were being covered by the apparently incoming tide. He alerted Brason, who had the tide table. He assured us that the tide was not due to turn for some hours yet.

Almost too late, I saw my towel disappearing as the tide started to come in. I looked anxiously at Roy. "Keep smiling as you swim into camera, look ha… "He now suddenly noticed the water starting to swirl over his feet and around the legs of the tripod holding the Arriflex. "CUT. Run for it!" he screamed.

They struggled to get the equipment off the beach. The tide was racing in and we knew that it would completely cover the whole area right up to the cliff face and a good way up the steps. Soaked to the skin and exhausted, we finally reached the top. It was a close run thing. A severe storm in the Atlantic had turned the tide early than usual.

For me, one night at the hotel, unable to dry clothing, have a decent meal or have a bit of peace and quiet was enough. I moved out and stayed with Doug in an old pub in Padstow.

Brason decided that filming on the beach was much too dangerous. George found an alternative: the hotel swimming pool. The three of us, bikini-clad, could frolic in the pool, come out and sit on a swinging hammock, drinking lemonade. Stuart dressed up as an elderly waiter with a drinks tray would fall into the pool, then cut to the three of us laughing at him. We spent a day just doing that. Jackie was told, at one point, to jump into the pool. This she did, splashing around with considerable verve until Roy noticed bits of white cotton wool floating in the water around her and stopped filming. "What the hell's that?" he screamed. It was Jackie's bust, she had filled the cups with cotton wool, and it had floated out.

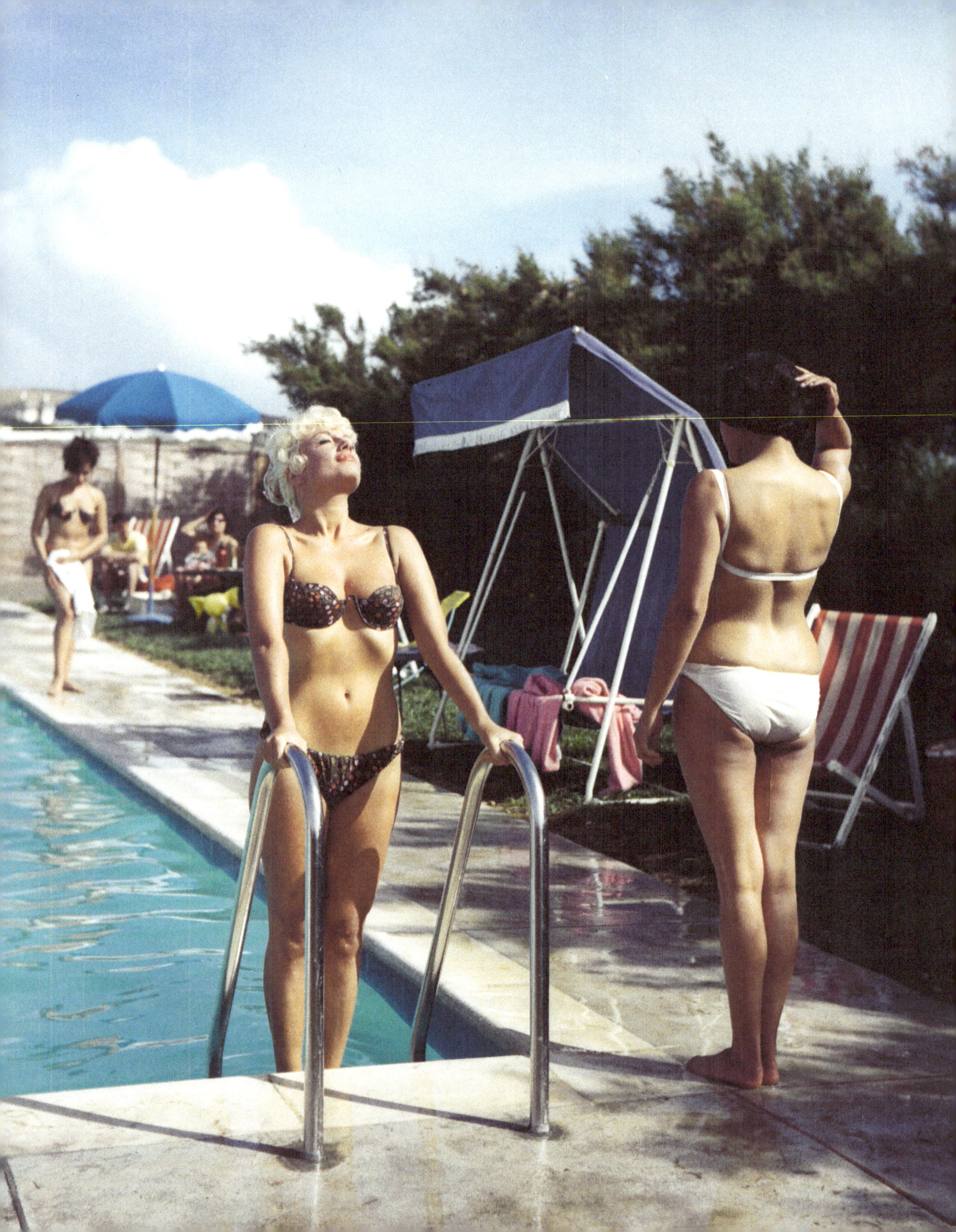

Watergate Bay

With Bedruthan Steps out, another location was needed. Watergate Bay was equally spectacular and much easier to reach. This then would be the setting for the scene where I discover Angela and Bridget in the nude.

A somewhat shaky sign reading "Terwyn Sun Club" was stuck in the sand; Bridget and Angela were ensconced behind a windbreak, me in a bikini. I walk around the rocks and find two naked women. Shock, horror and embarrassment! We made the dialogue up as we went along. Roy was not shooting sound, except as a guide track. Although they are nudists, I find them friendly. They rapidly convince me that to be ashamed of one's body is surely unnatural and wrong. That there is nothing immoral about enjoying the feeling of complete physical freedom that nudity brings. I climb the nearest chunk of rock and wave to my two friends to come over. The weather was not good that day. A brisk wind was blowing and it was overcast.

We went through the motions, for it would have to be re-shot on a better day. Bridget standing in the surf was told to turn left and run up the beach. She

Left: The hotel pool into which Pamela accidentally pushes Stuart the waiter in was a hastily improvised added scene.

Below: Pamela Green swimming in the same hotel pool. It was decided that the pool was a much safer environment to film the swimming sequences than in the rough surf of the North Cornwall coast.

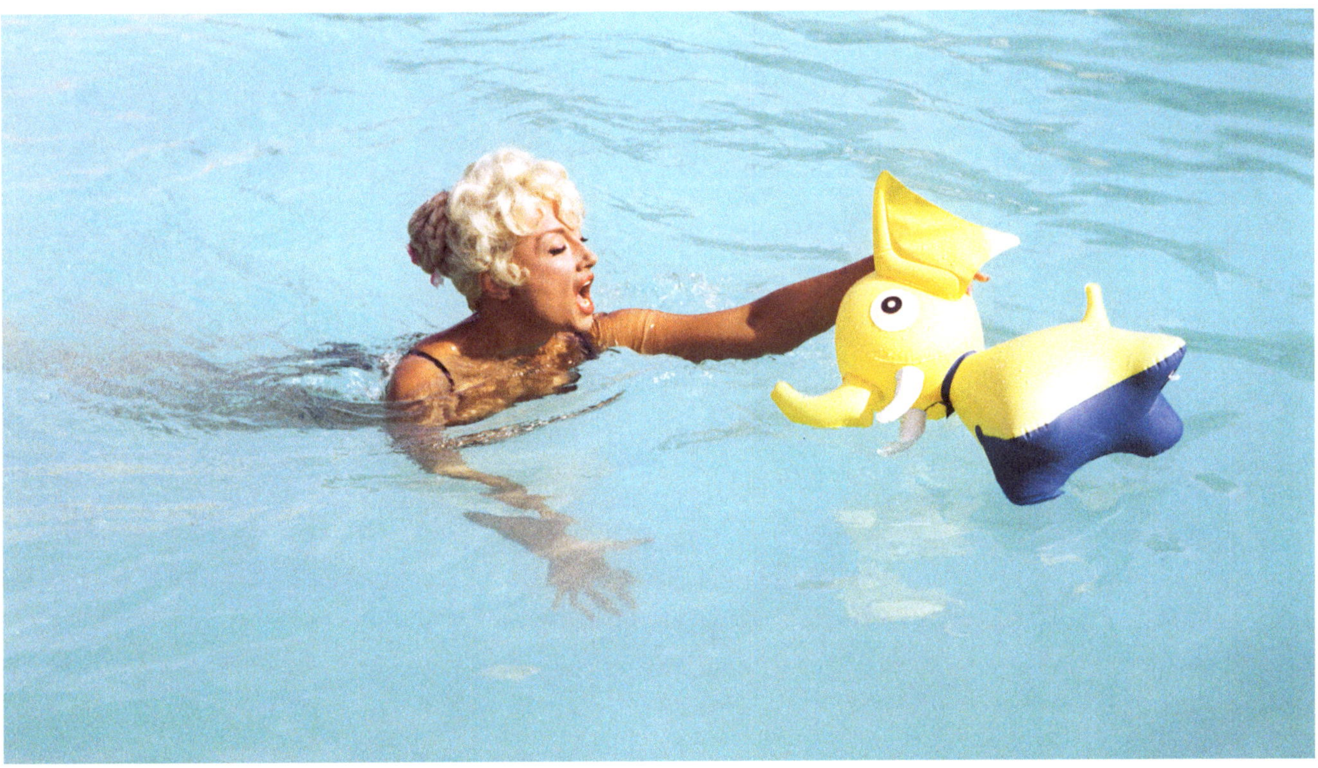

turned right and ran straight into the sea. Roy, by now had also had enough, “Oh, let her go” he said wearily, “She doesn’t know her left from her right”.

Right: Pamela Green waves to the crew. Although the sky is blue and the sun appears to be shining, the reality was that the cold and the wind made filming on the beach more an endurance test than a happy outing.

Two apparitions were spotted making their way across the beach. Klinger and Tenser had arrived to see us working. Nattily dressed in matching blazers and sporting colourful ties, trousers with knife-sharp creases and highly polished shoes, they surveyed the scene of five blue skinned girls shivering with cold and a fed-up looking crew. The sand blew in their faces and the spray soaked their shiny shoes. George came panting up clutching his beach ball. They gazed at all this, then remembering an appointment with a large gin and tonic they left and retired to the nearest pub before returning to London and civilisation.

The final shots, according to the rough-shooting schedule were “A fairly long pictorial sequence of sand, sea and nude shots”. Then with a note of pessimism creeping in “entirely dictated by conditions as available” ending hopefully with, “Underwater nude swimming shots. IF POSSIBLE.”

Both crew and cast rejected that one straight out of hand. The weather had closed in. North Cornwall beaches are the most spectacular in the country, but can also be the coldest. Now with the wind whipping up the surf, the flying sand stinging our bare flesh, we raced into a distinctly unfriendly Atlantic. “Splash about and swim”. George was still attached to his beloved loudhailer. Numbly we splashed, swim we dared not, even Jackie’s customary enthusiasm seemed to have left her.

“Come out and run back to your towels” hailed George. This was a long shot showing an empty beach and five nude girls running towards the camera. Ever mindful of the censors, the shot had to be as far away as possible. In the finished results we appear so small, we could have been wearing woolly hats and long-johns. A cloak of mist finally eclipsed the light. So the “pretty-pretty shot of sunset to end sequence”, joined the legion of the lost: Jamaica Inn, Woolacombe Beach and Exmoor.

The beach scene was finally re-created at Presbury’s Studios in Dean Street. A bright blue backing with the windbreak and some sand on the floor. It didn’t match the outdoor sequence in any way, shape or form.

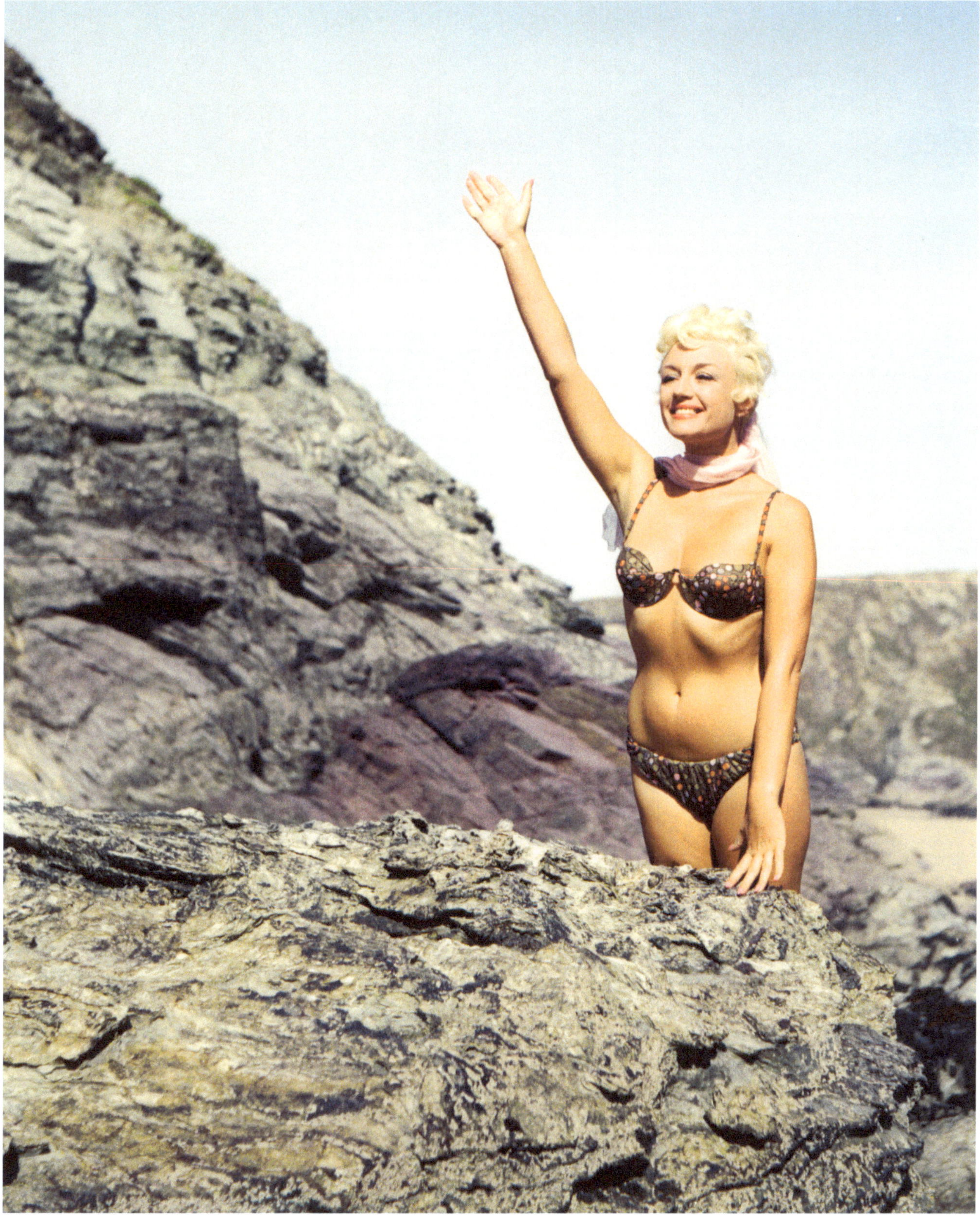

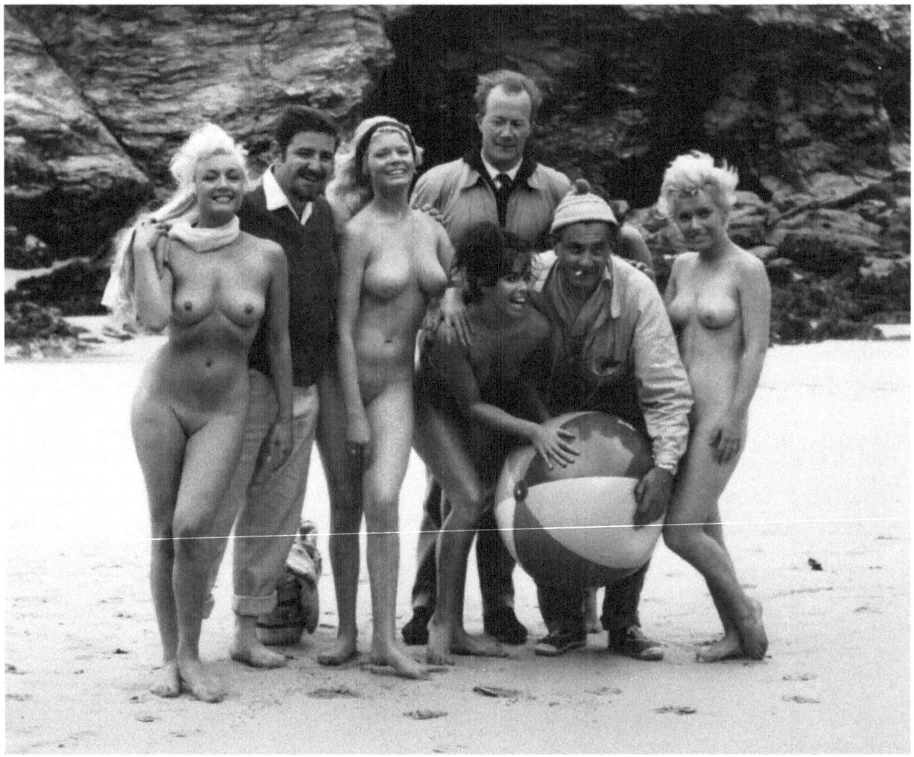

Right: Cast and crew on the beach in North Cornwall during a break in filming.

Falmouth Again

George wanted to film more footage of us on the boat, so we went back to Falmouth. Wanting to get some long distance shots George filmed us from another boat. Doug was in our boat to take stills of me, Petrina, Jackie and Stuart. As our boats drifted apart, George shouted through the loudhailer. "Run up and down the boat". "Wave, all of you!" "Stuart, pretend you've caught a shark". George's voice grew fainter over the ever-widening gap. We could just about hear him bellow out the song "If you knew Susie as I know Susie… ". Brason sat in the stern of the boat with his back to them, gloomily watching Falmouth disappearing aft.

We had to return to London the next day as we were to start shooting the scenes at Spielplatz Sun Club the following week. We were already behind schedule.

Spielplatz

Spielplatz was just the same as when I first went there with fellow art student Fay Smith in 1949, to get an even tan. I recognised the very place where I stood and posed for the Miss Venus Beauty Competition, which I won eleven years before. The club was founded in 1929 by Charles Macaskie and his wife Dorothy. I was friends with their daughter Iseult.

In the script, the naturist club is meant to be near the beach in Cornwall. The sequences shot there were constricted by the lack of scenery. The wooden huts, the small pool with its' murky water, a few trees and the worn grass area (used for tennis, badminton, or any other game involving a net) didn't readily lend themselves to people that wanted to paint with light.

The members were all nice people and helpful, but photographically the club was poor. As far as Trevelyan was concerned, this was the grand finale, the whole point of the film. We were to be introduced to the President of the club who was

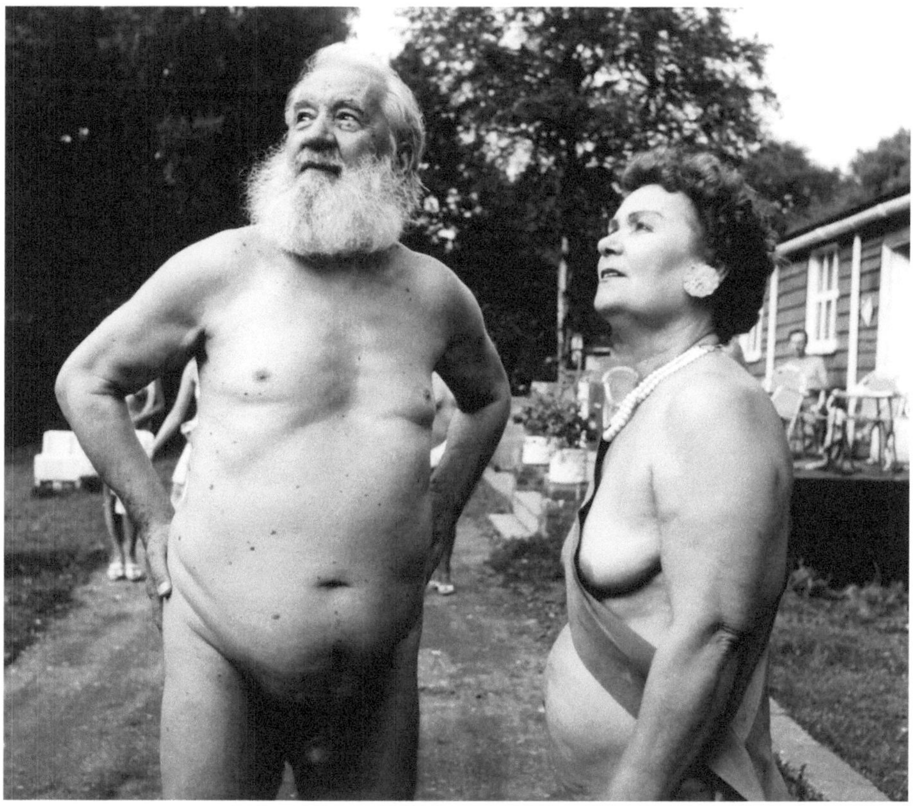

Left: Nudist pioneers Charles and Dorothy Macaskie, who founded the Speilplatz naturist club.

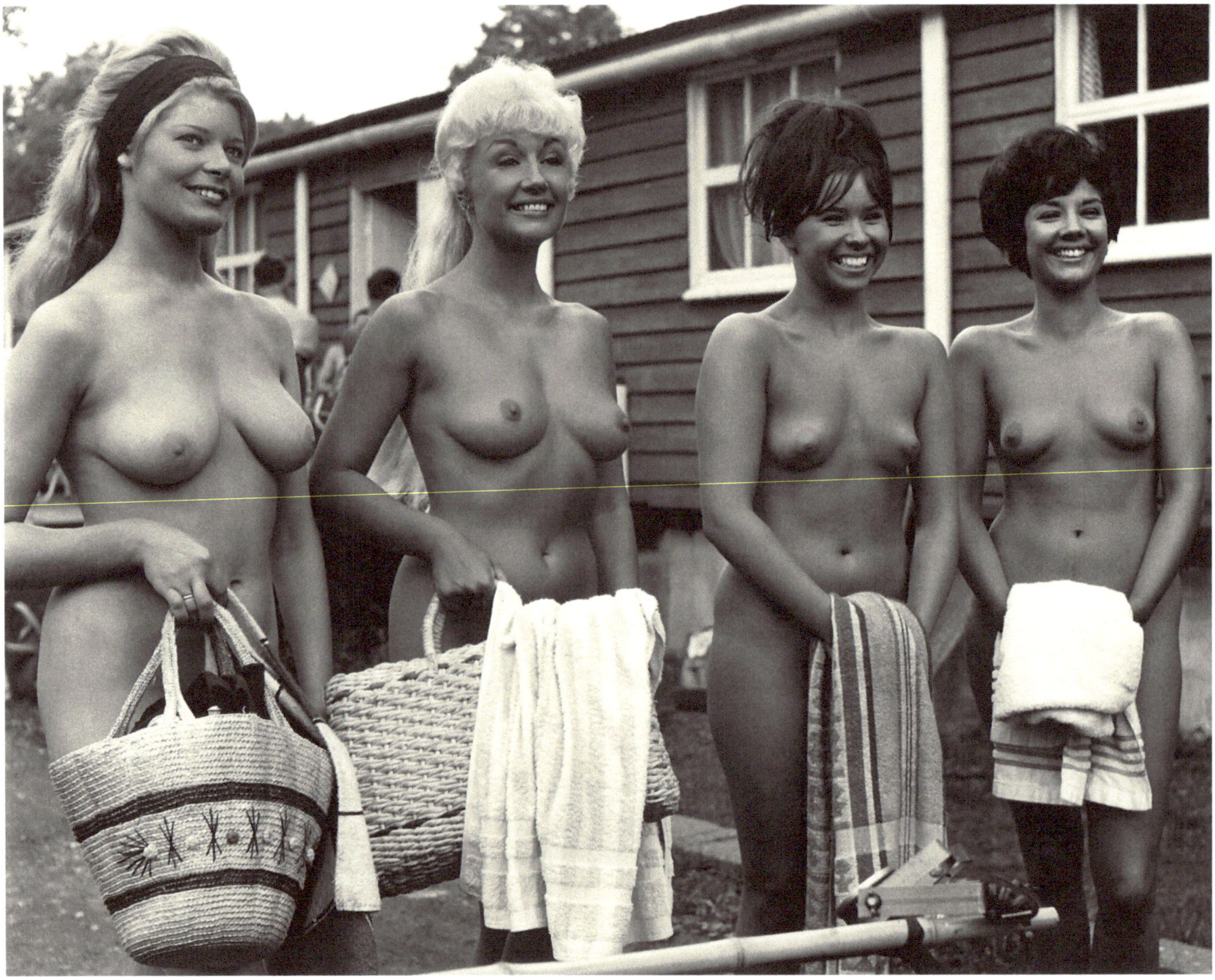

Above: Bridget Leonard, Pamela Green, Jackie salt and Petrina Forsyth – towels at the ready to keep the censors happy.

to give us a guided tour of the camp. Charles Macaskie, however, was elderly and frail and lived in a heated caravan, so appearances with him were naturally brief. His wife, Dorothy, who seemed impervious to the elements and jauntily wearing a blue satin sash and two rows of beads, took his place.

With the censors in mind we all had towels and baskets held firmly across our fronts as if they were glued to us – at least we didn't have to wave. A personable young male actor was hired to walk about with us. The actual members were asked to stand around discreetly in-groups and with the ubiquitous towels to hand, held fore or aft depending on the camera angle. In make-up the first day, I noticed that our male actor, apart from having shaved off all his pubic hair, was making up his 'dangly bits' with Max Factor Pancake make-up!

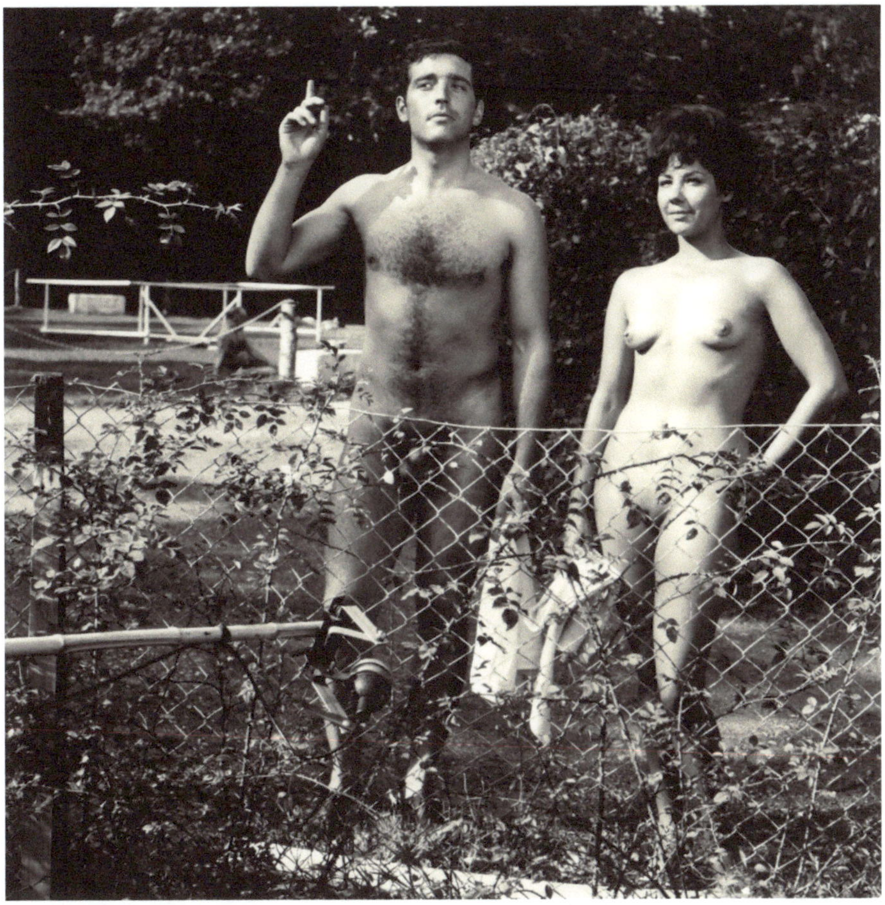

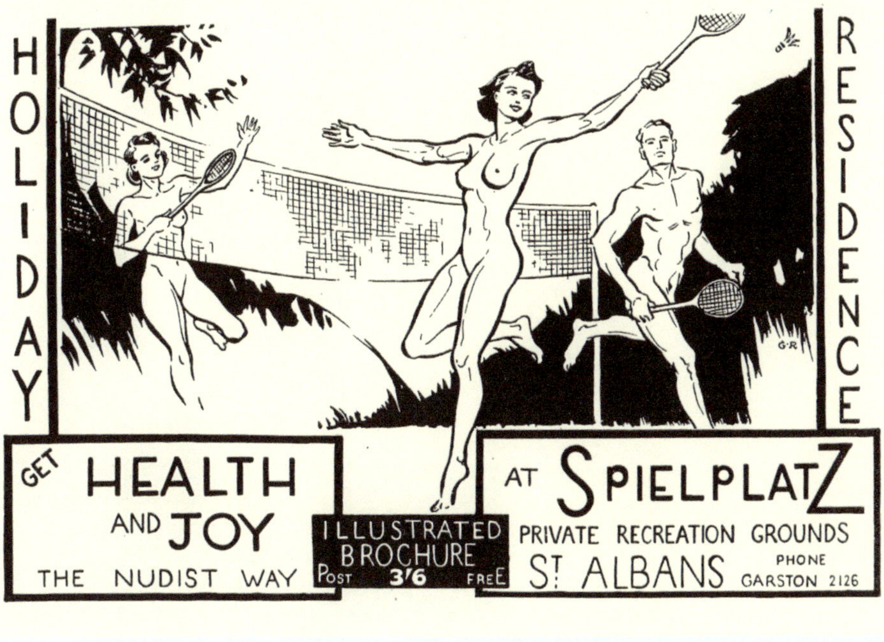

Top Left: Male model and Petrina Forysth with strategically placed rose leaves on the wire fence hiding their "offending parts".

Bottom Left: Magazine ad for Speilplatz Naturist Club.

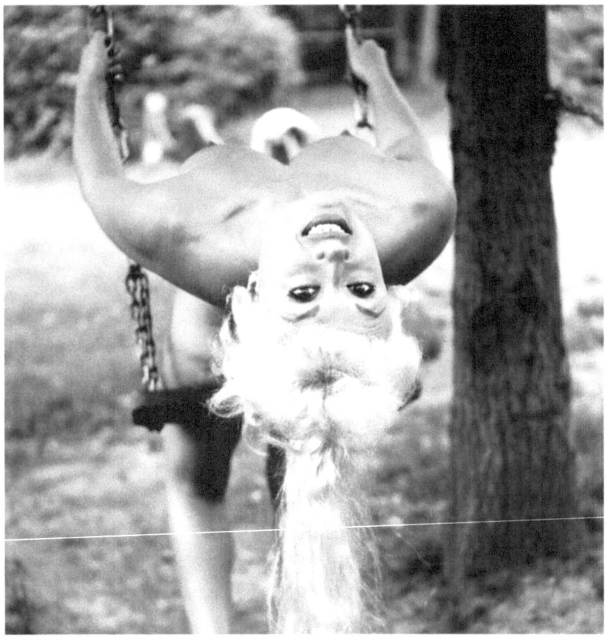

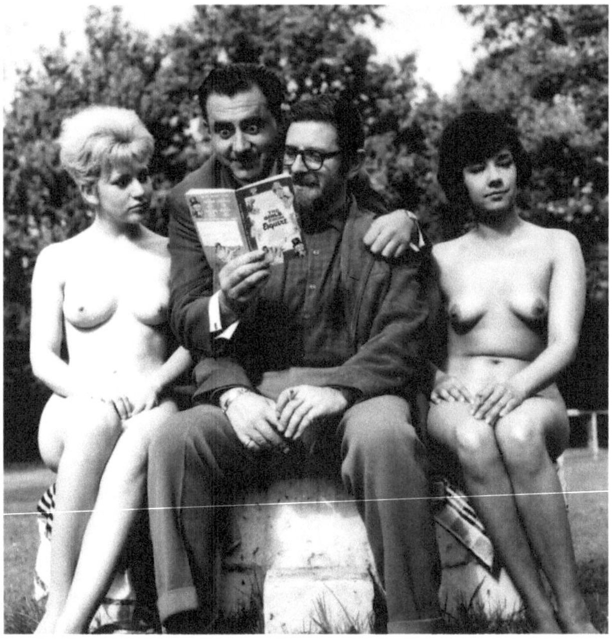

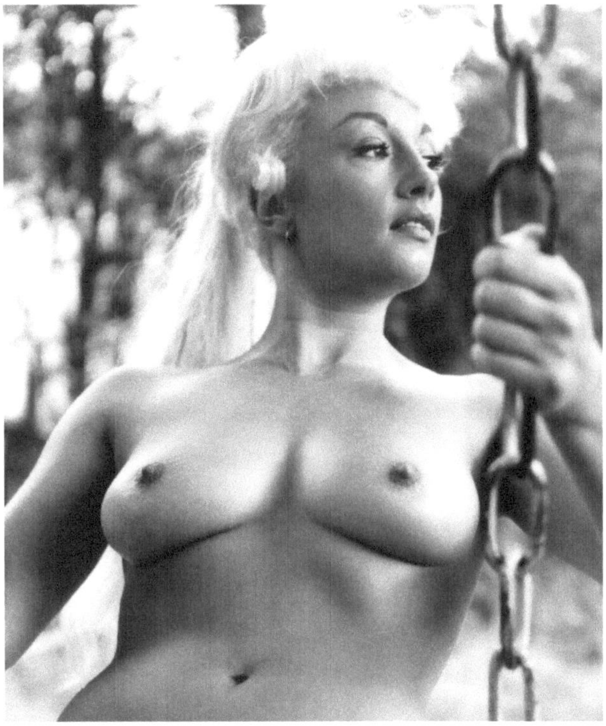

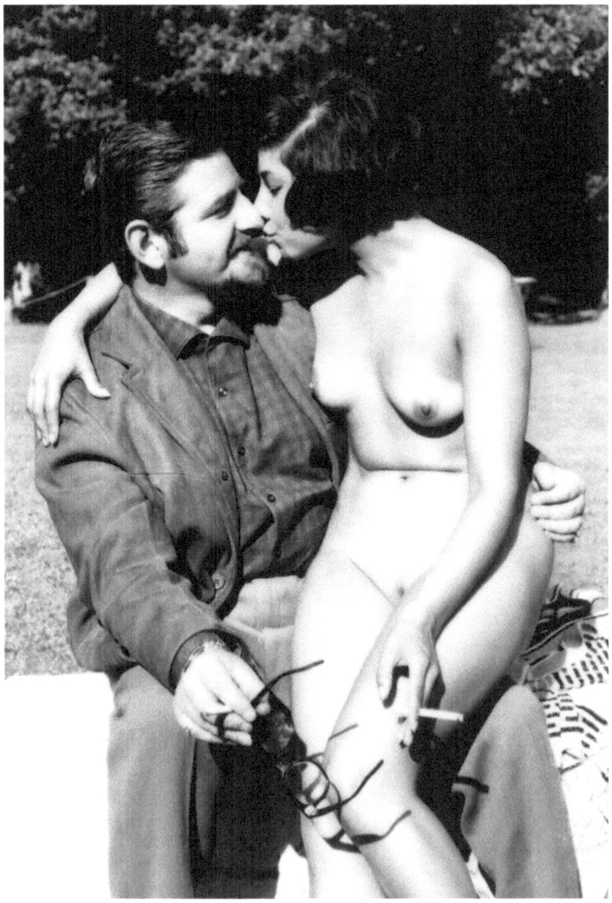

Top and Bottom Left: Pamela tries out the swing.

Top Right: Angela Jones and Petrina Forsyth sit patiently while Harrison Marks and Roy Pointer enjoy the book, *The Girls from Esquire.*

Bottom right: Director Harrison Marks flirts with Petrina Forsyth.

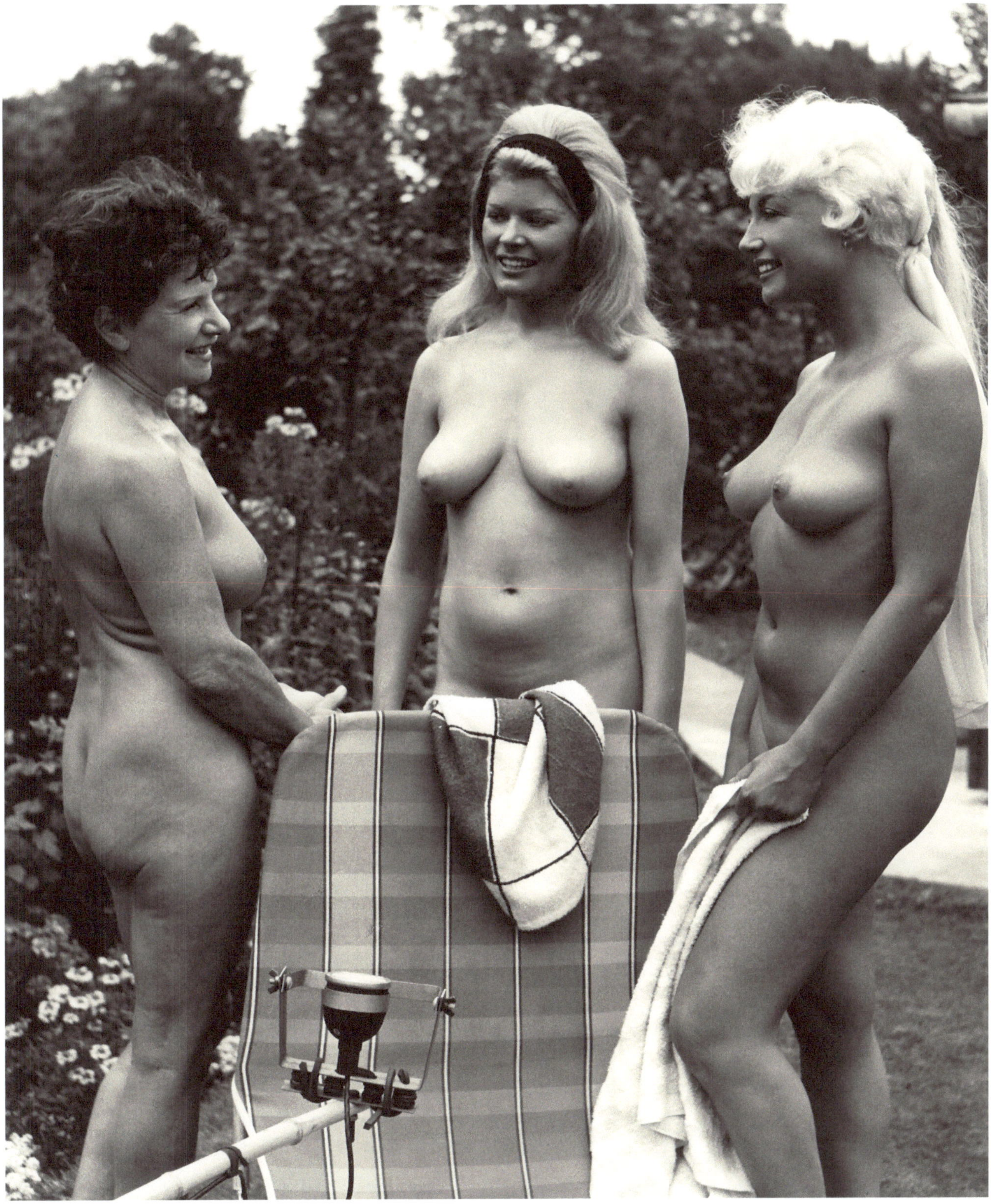

Above: Bridget Leonard and Pamela Green chat to a Kitty Jones, a long term resident at Speilplatz.

Below and right: The girls outside the rather austere clubhouse at Spielplatz enjoying a drink and a chat.

Although armed with a towel and instructions to keep his "bits" covered, he had a tendency to forget and let the towel drop. In the publicity shots there he was, offending "bits" in full view. They were standing behind an open wire fence which came up to their waists, a rose was climbing up one side of the wire, so I extended the rose and incorporated the offending parts into the leaves.

The final shots were a 15 minute sequences of camp activities. We quickly exhausted the table tennis, the swimming and the quoits. Doug did a series of stills of me on a swing. We were filmed talking to the residents and admiring their gardens. After that we all left, getting into the Buick and driving off, waving, supposedly silhouetted against the sunset. George seemed to be very fond of sunsets, it was his misfortune that there were never any.

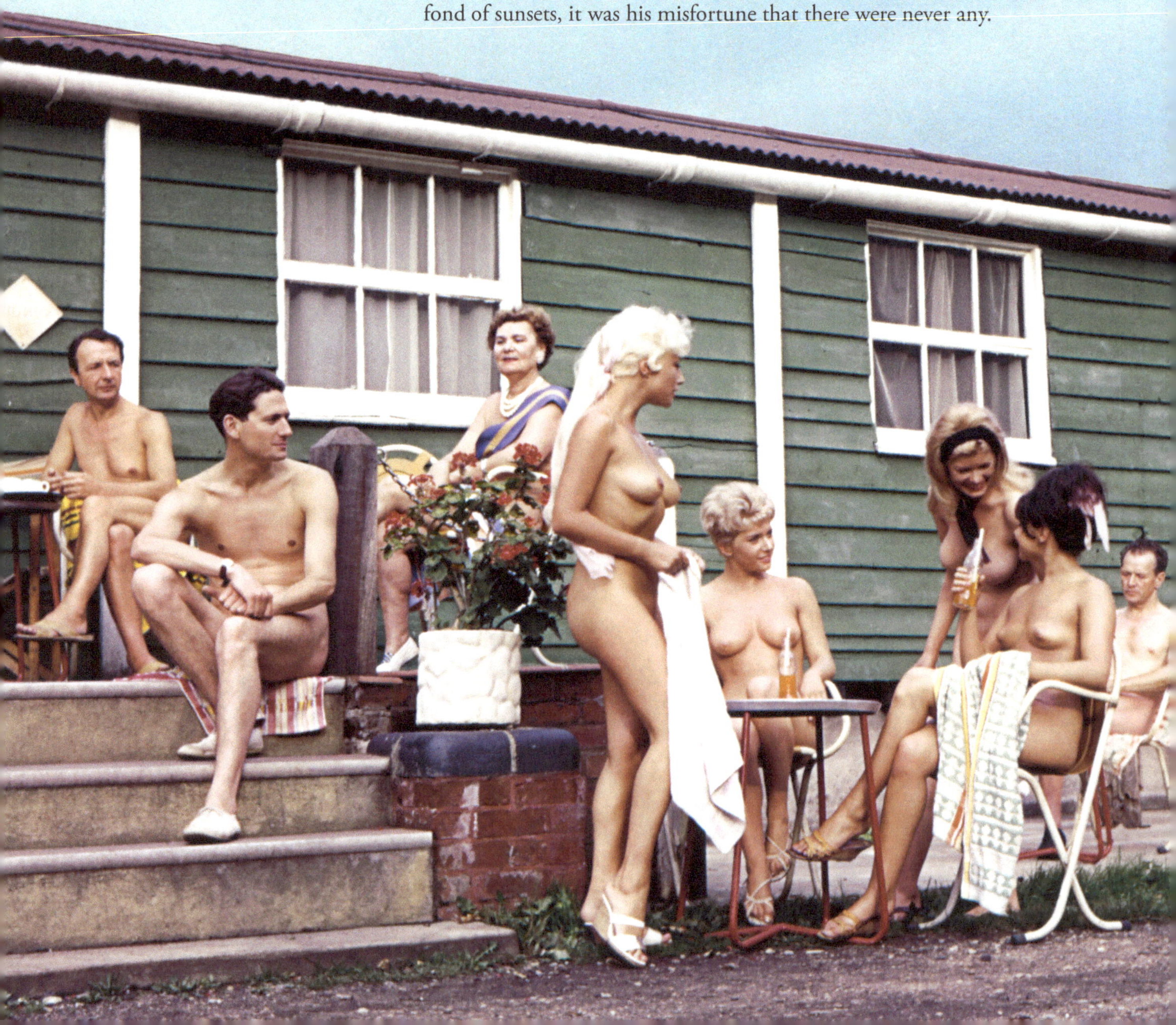

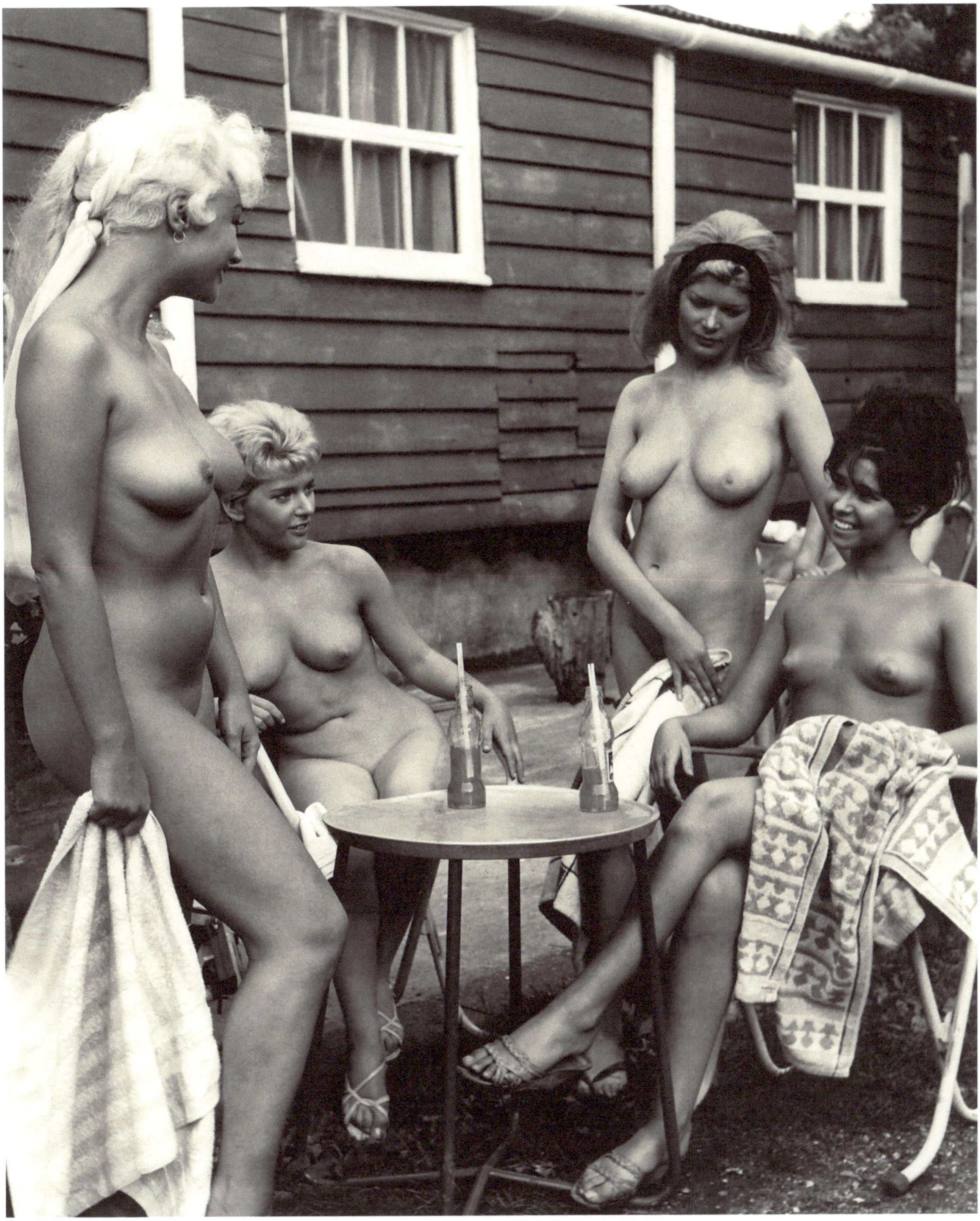

Back to the start

As seems normal in filming, we began in the middle and worked our way to either end. We now went back to the beginning of the film, the bit that establishes the various characters.

Pam, the dancer, and Petrina, who works in a solicitor's office, share a flat. The opening shot shows the two of us examining a map of Cornwall. I have just been filmed coming out of the shower. Petrina, in a baby-doll negligee, and me wrapped up in a bath towel, discuss our route. The hour is obviously late. The censors, however, maintained that two girls sharing a flat could be lesbians and cut out that entire scene. The film starts with us driving off with no explanation.

Right: Pamela Green stepping out of the shower in one of the opening shots of the film.

Far right: Pamela in a bath towel and Petrina in a negligee in the supposed lesbian scene. Apparently, two young women dressed this way and looking at a map of Cornwall could be mistaken for lesbians according to the censor. The whole scene was cut from the finished film.

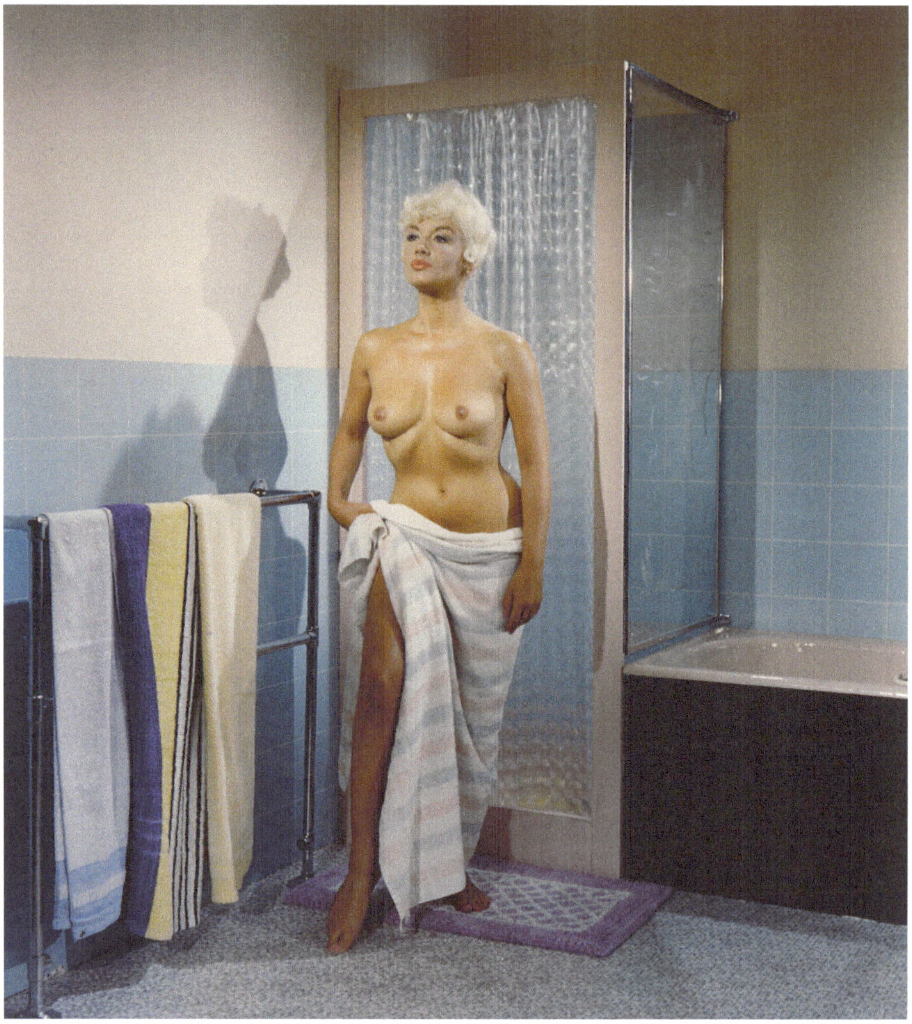

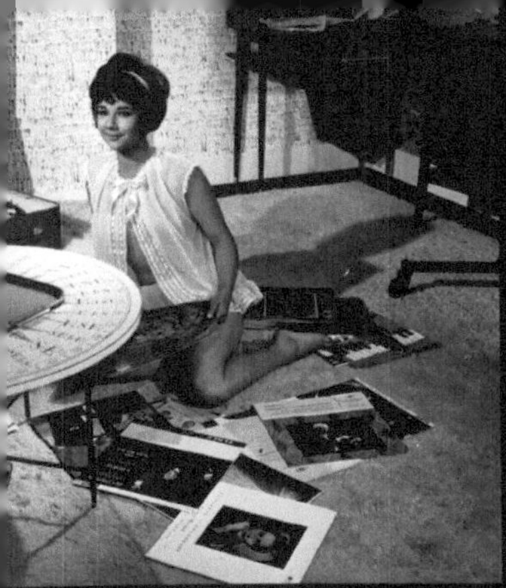
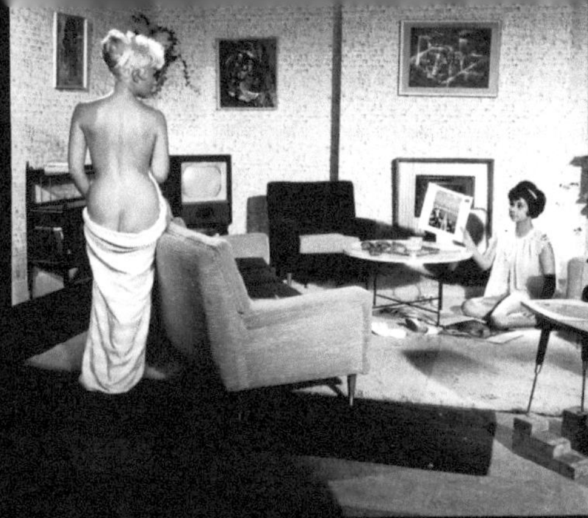
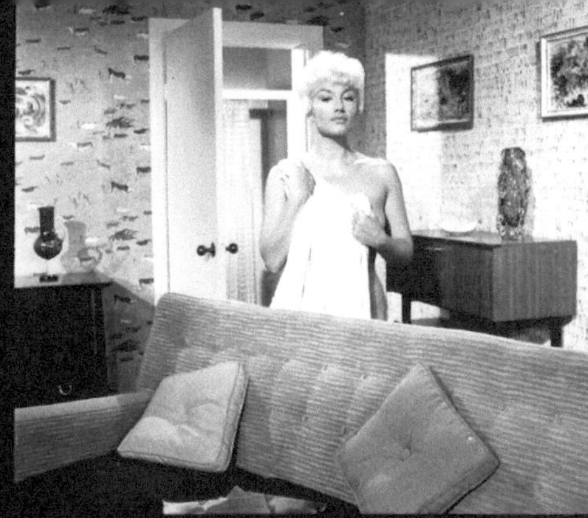
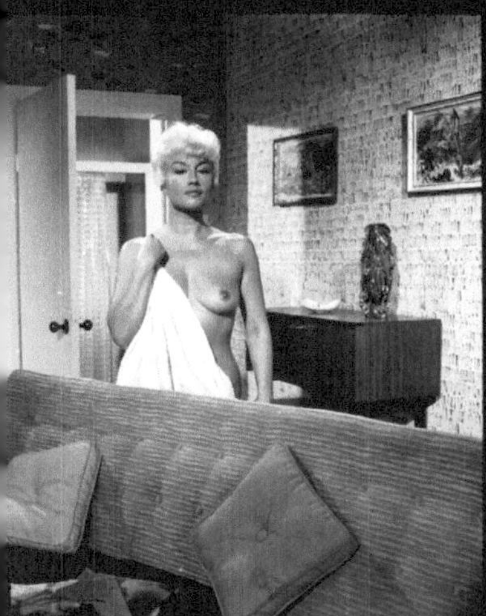
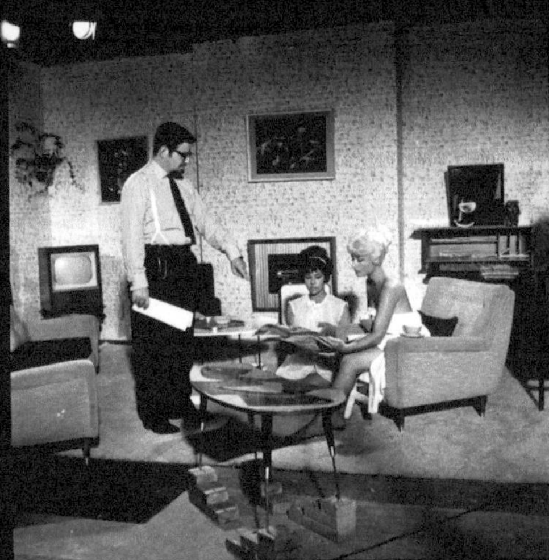
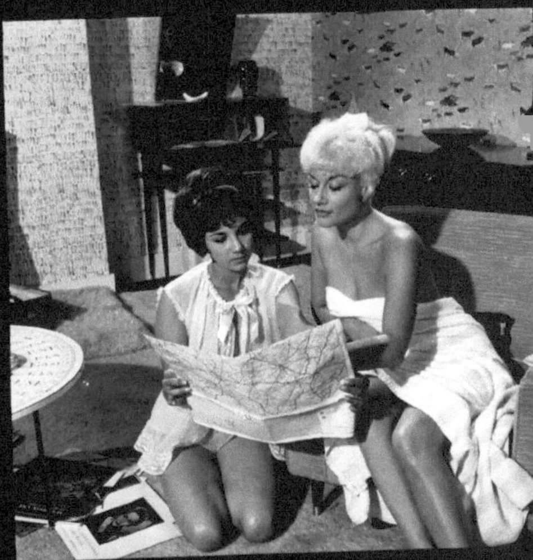
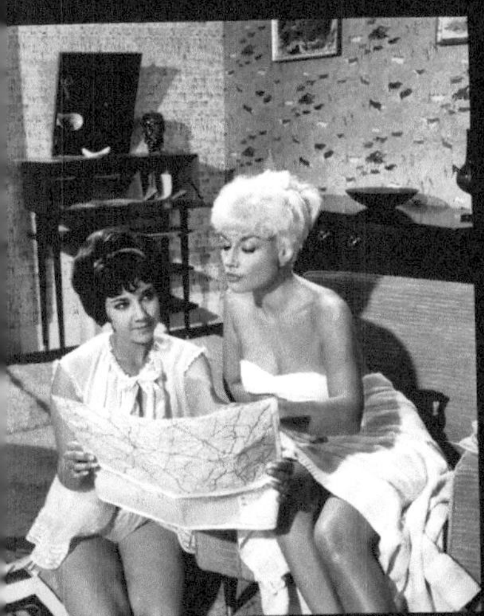
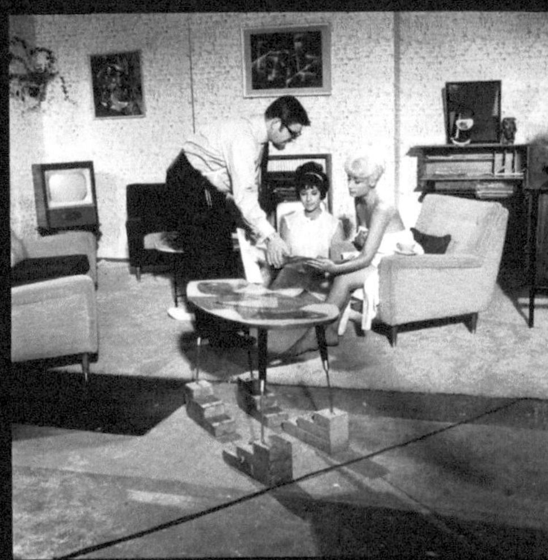
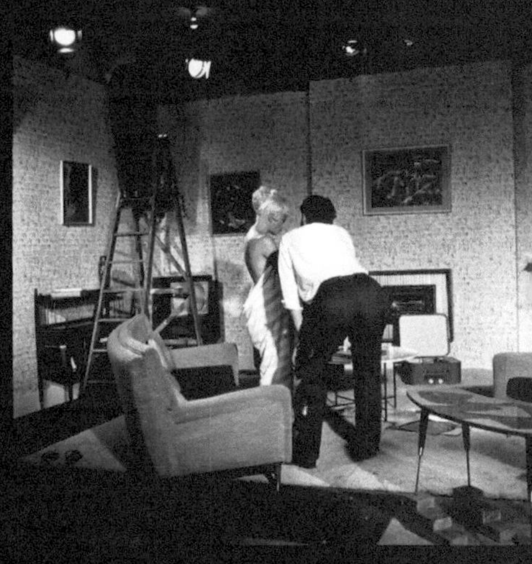
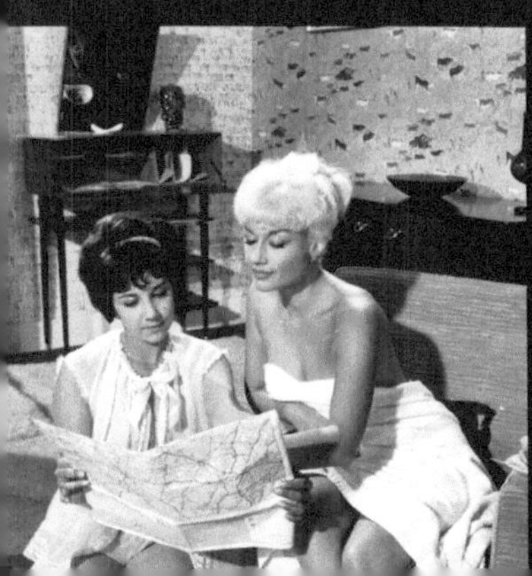
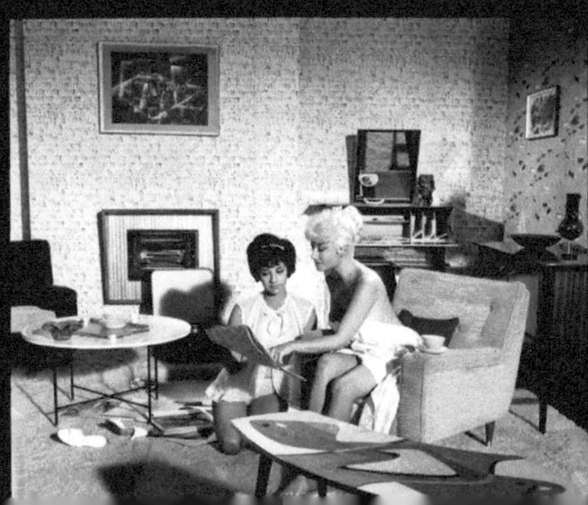
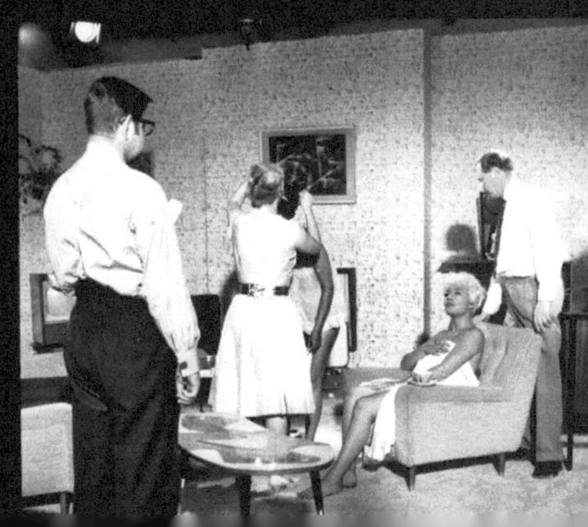

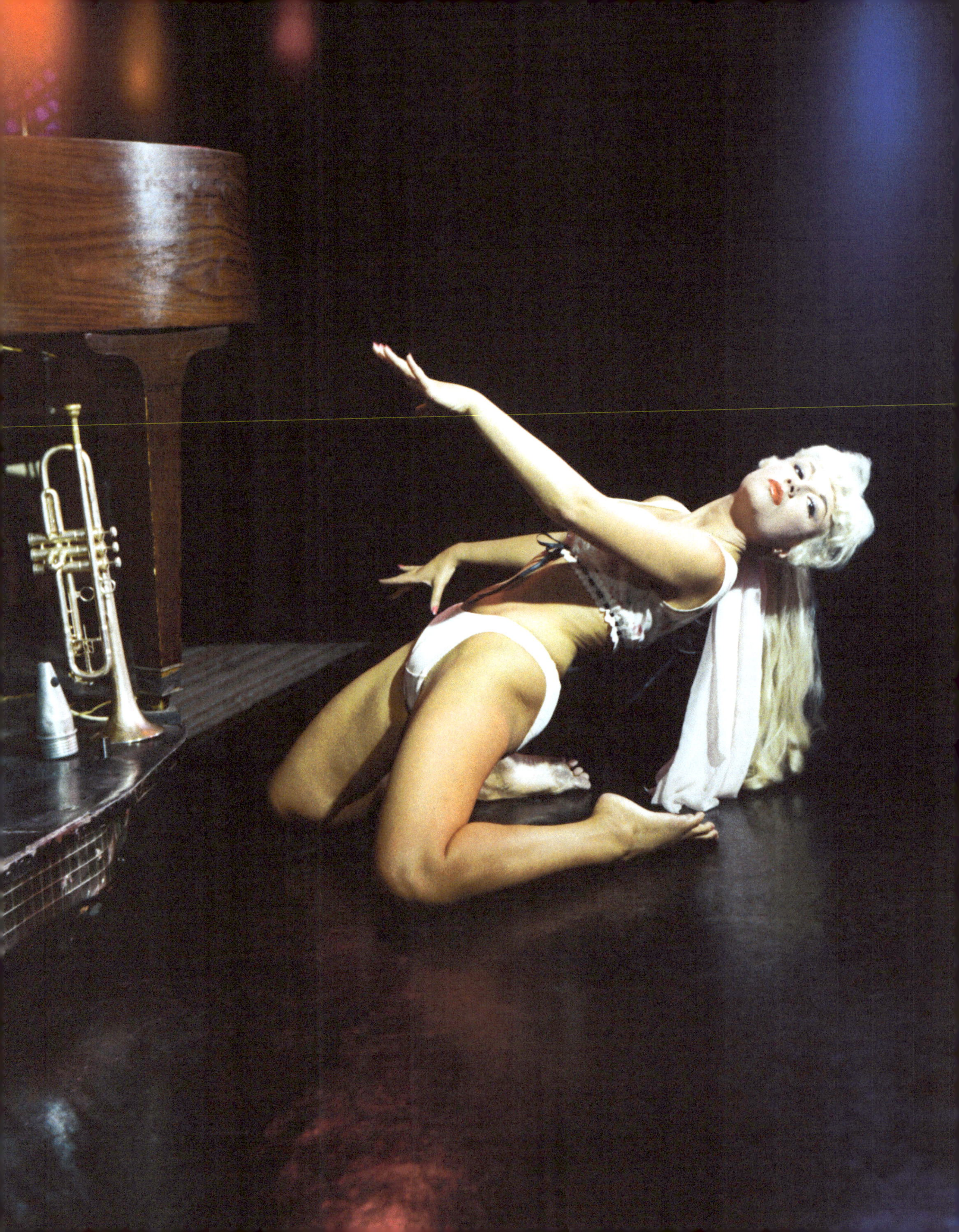

Next came the scenes of me rehearsing on stage and leaving the theatre and getting into the Buick. The theatre chosen was the Golders Green Hippodrome – I am seen leaving the stage door. The actual dance sequence was shot in the Gargoyle Club in Soho.

Re-shoot at Presbury's Studios

We sat on the studio floor, on yellow sand in front of the windbreak, behind which was a bright blue backing. Our make-up perfect and not a hair out of place, and so it stayed as the tight budget could not stretch to a wind machine.

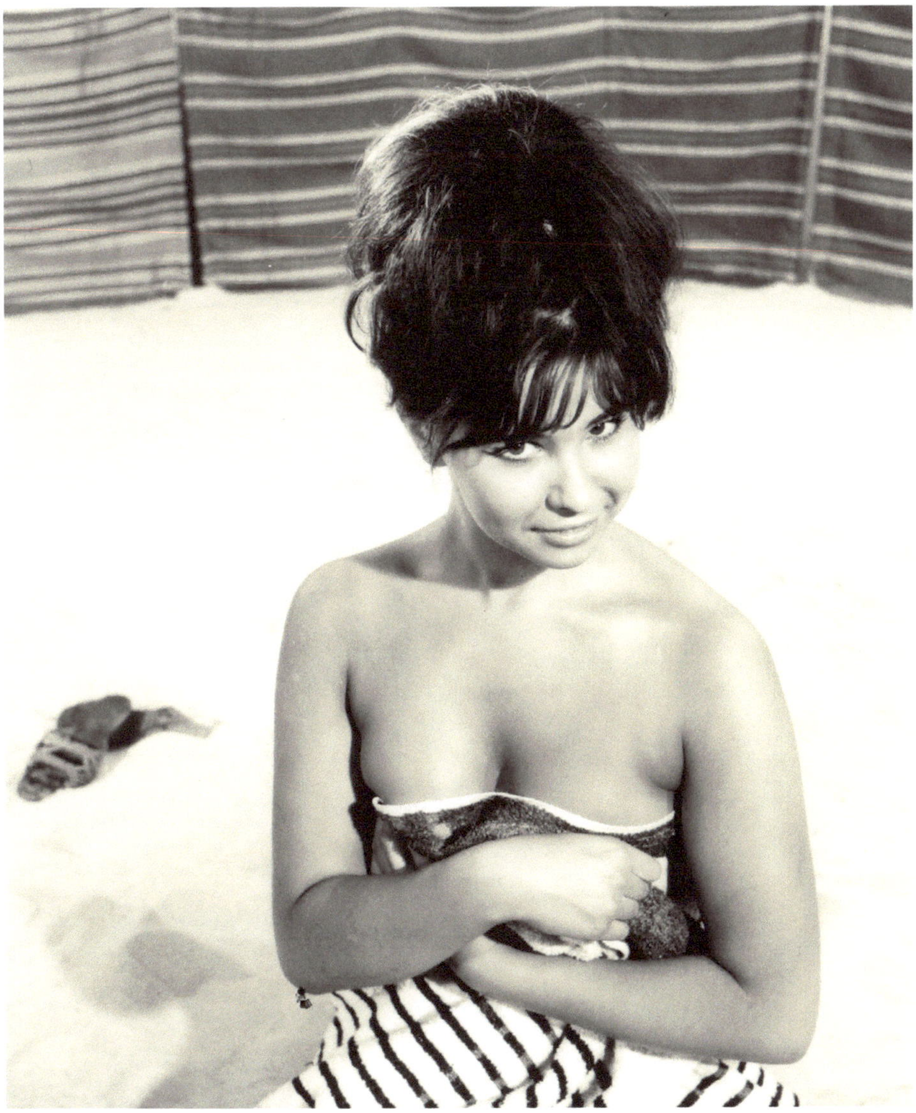

Far left: Pamela Green dancing at the Gargoyle Club in Meard's Street, Soho. At the time the club was run by Michael Klinger. It was founded in 1925 and had been the epitome of decadent glamour but by the 1950s it had become a drinking den and a haunt for artists. Francis Bacon and Lucian Freud were regulars.

Left: Jackie Salt on the re-created beach at Presburys Studios in Dean Street.

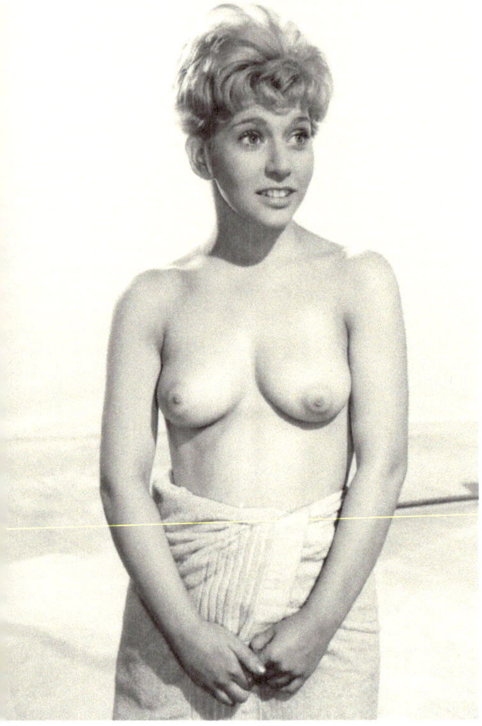

All in place, Roy lit us. This is where we were to discuss naturism. We all looked blank. By now, it was 1 pm, the unit broke for lunch, and all went to the pub in Macclesfield Street. "Not you lot". Brason called us back. "You can spend your lunch hour learning your dialogue". "John", I said, "There is no dialogue, there has never been any dialogue. Furthermore, he who should have written it is at this moment stuffing himself with smoked salmon sandwiches and enjoying a large drink. I suggest that instead of nagging us, you go and find him". Grimly Brason left the studio, hauled George away from his lunch and bid him to write.

That afternoon we received our few lines, each on separate pieces of paper. The four girls learnt the lines they had to say, but not when or in what order. After endless, "Oh, is it me now?" and "I've forgotten. What do I say?", patience was exhausted.

Slowly and laboriously, we toiled on. The lure of the sea, sun and sand proved overwhelming, as we longed to move free, as nature intended. Converted to naturism, we threw away our bikini tops. Petrina and I dropped ours somewhat

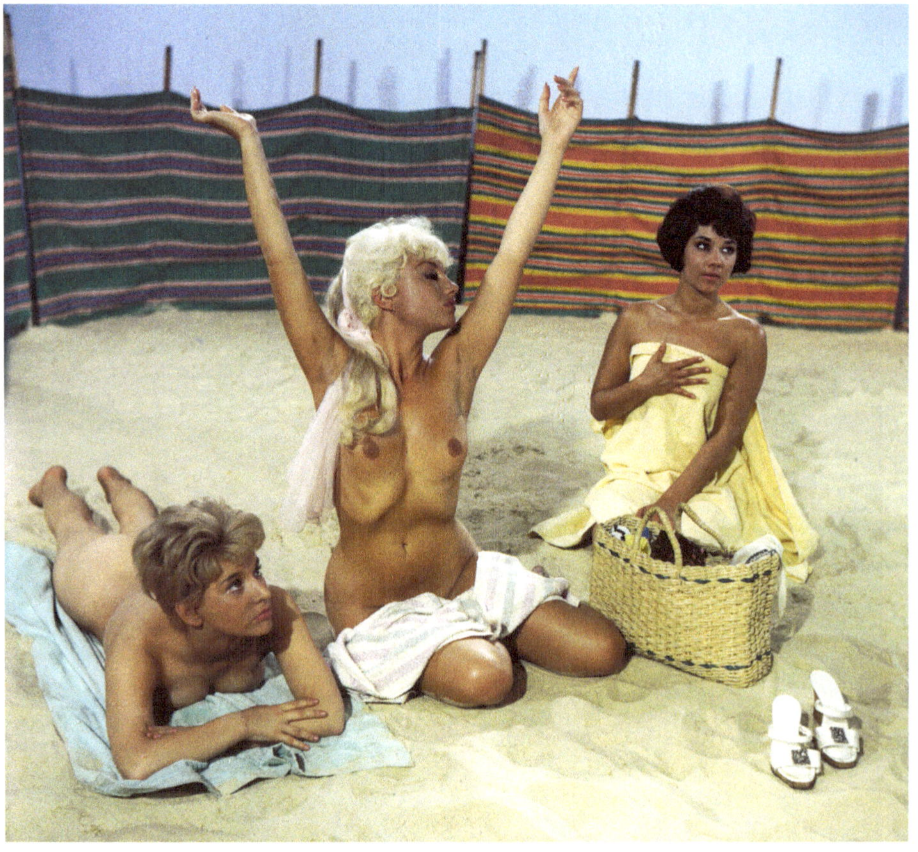

Above: Angela Jones.

Right: Angela Jones, Pamela Green and Petrina Forsyth basking in the studio lights in Dean Street.

Far Right: Bridget Leonard. The film's publicity material states that "born in Donegal, Ireland, Bridget spent her early years in a small village until she was fifteen and spoke no other tongue than her native Gaelic. Three years ago, however, a talent scout working with a Swedish film company in Ireland spotted her, and on their return to Sweden she went with them and worked in several films. Bridget first came to England just a year ago to learn English and to study at one of our drama schools. Introduced to Harrison Marks who was very much impressed by her sparkling beauty, she was signed-up to participate in *Naked – As Nature Intended*." Vital statistics 38"-24"-36".

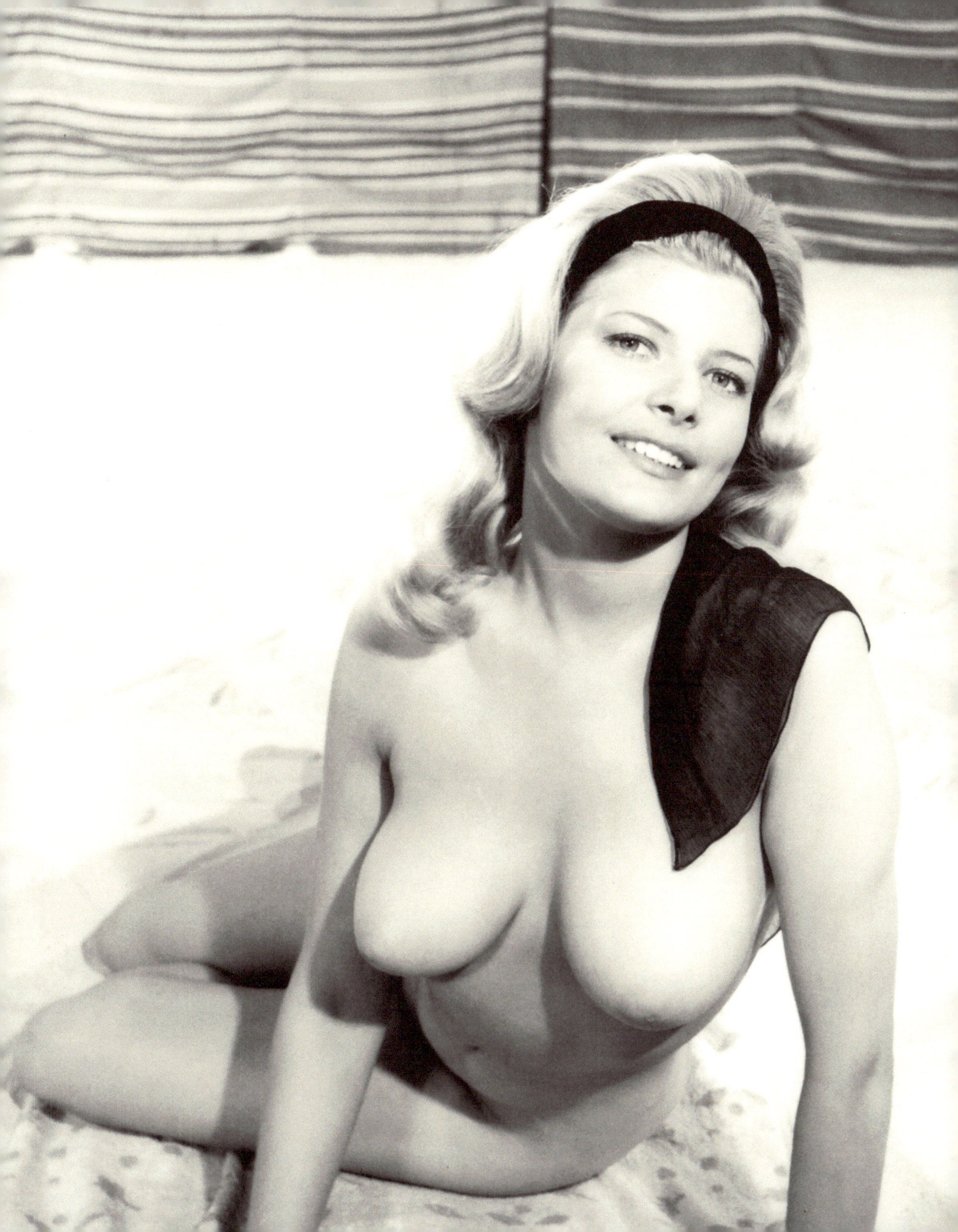

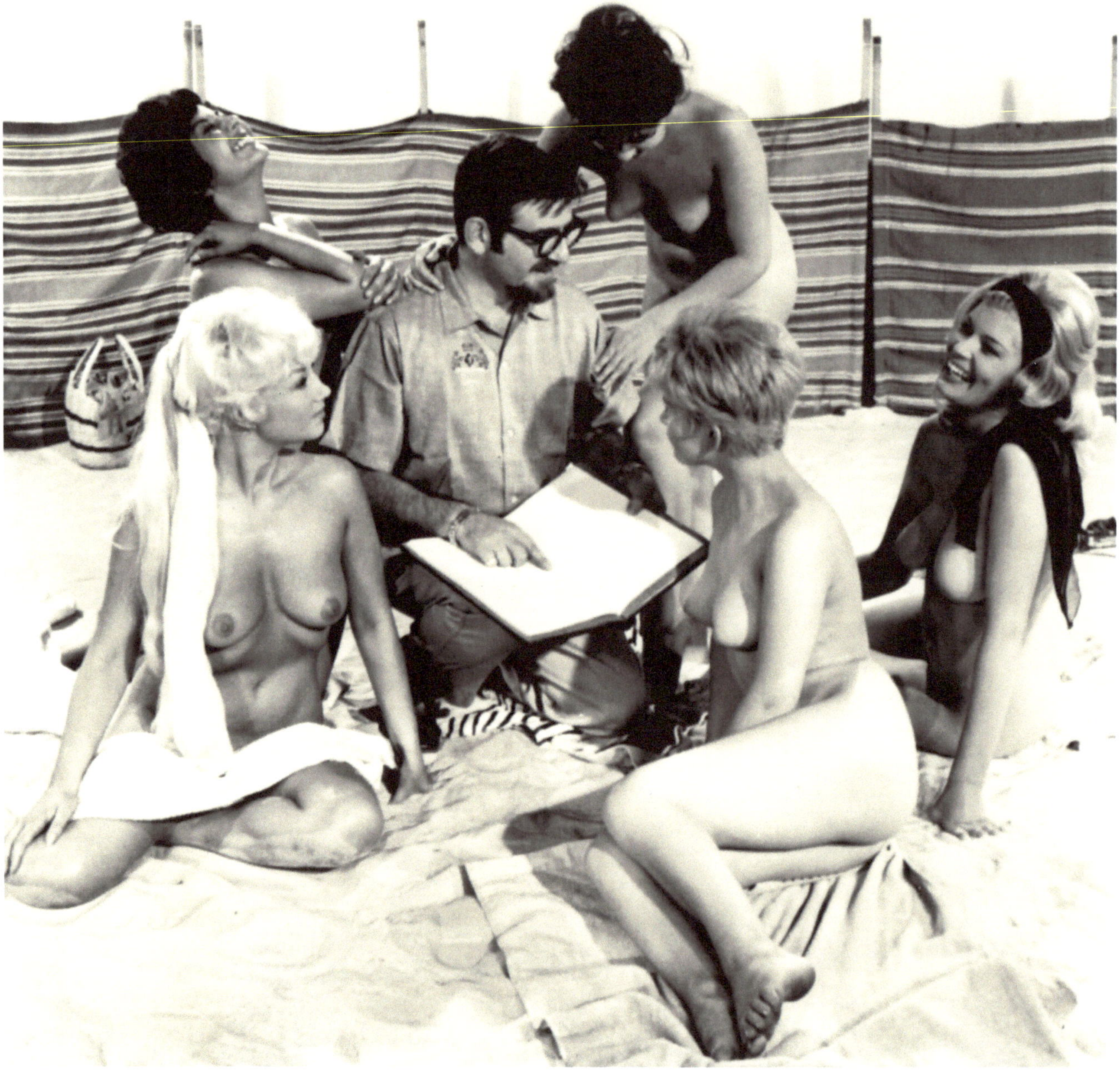

indifferently but Jackie threw hers away with a wild "Whey!", disclosing her extremely small bust. She was the only one with any animation or enthusiasm in the entire film.

In the script, we collect Jackie from her home, so a location was needed for that, plus someone to take the part of Jackie's mother. George's mother unwittingly remarked one day that her neighbour had a smiling dog. This then was the location for Jackie's departure. The owner of the dog was cast in the role of Jackie's mother. We all arrived in Wembley with the Buick. George's mother had the sense to keep well out of the way, but Bert, her better half was cast as the nosy neighbour. Jackie came out of the house followed by her Mum. The dog sat up and smiled. Jackie got into the car with Petrina and me, and waving, we all drove off. Filming was finally finished.

Far left: A relaxed moment as George Harrison Marks takes the girls through their few lines of dialogue.

Below left: Petrina, Pamela, Bert and Jackie.

Below right: Bert, playing Jackie's father, waves goodbye as the girls set out on their holiday. Although this scene is one of the early sequences of the film it was the last to be actually shot.

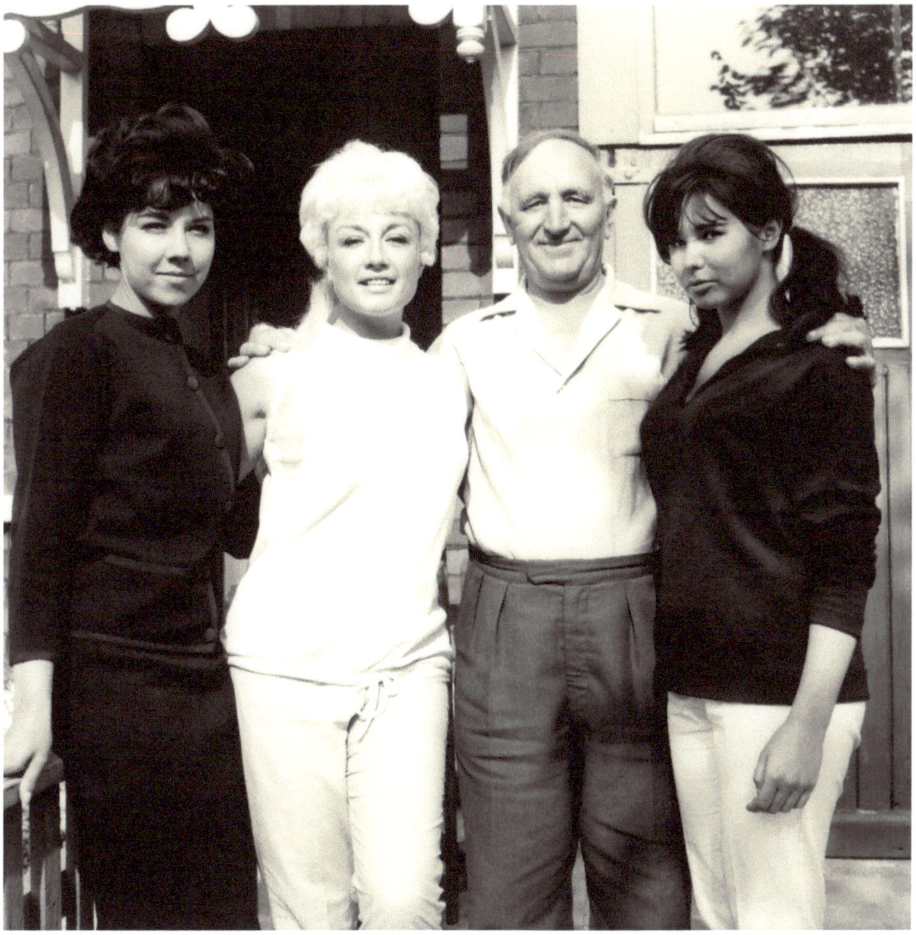

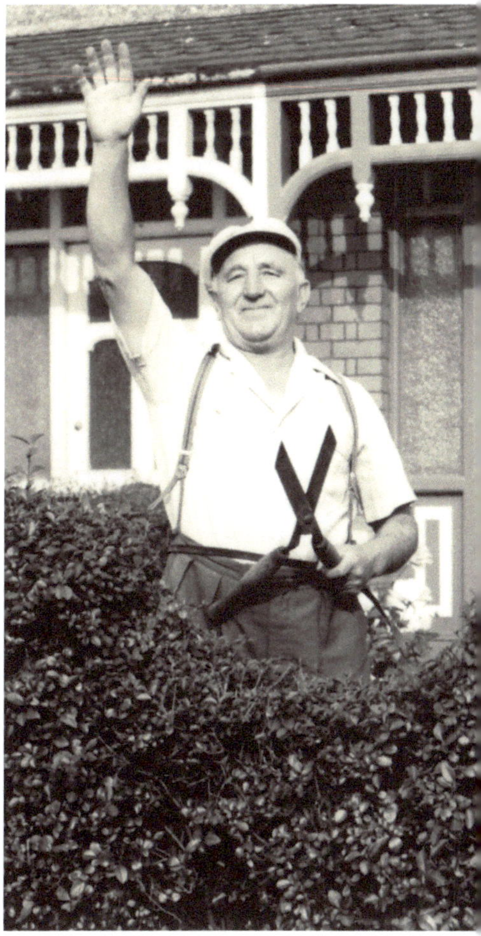

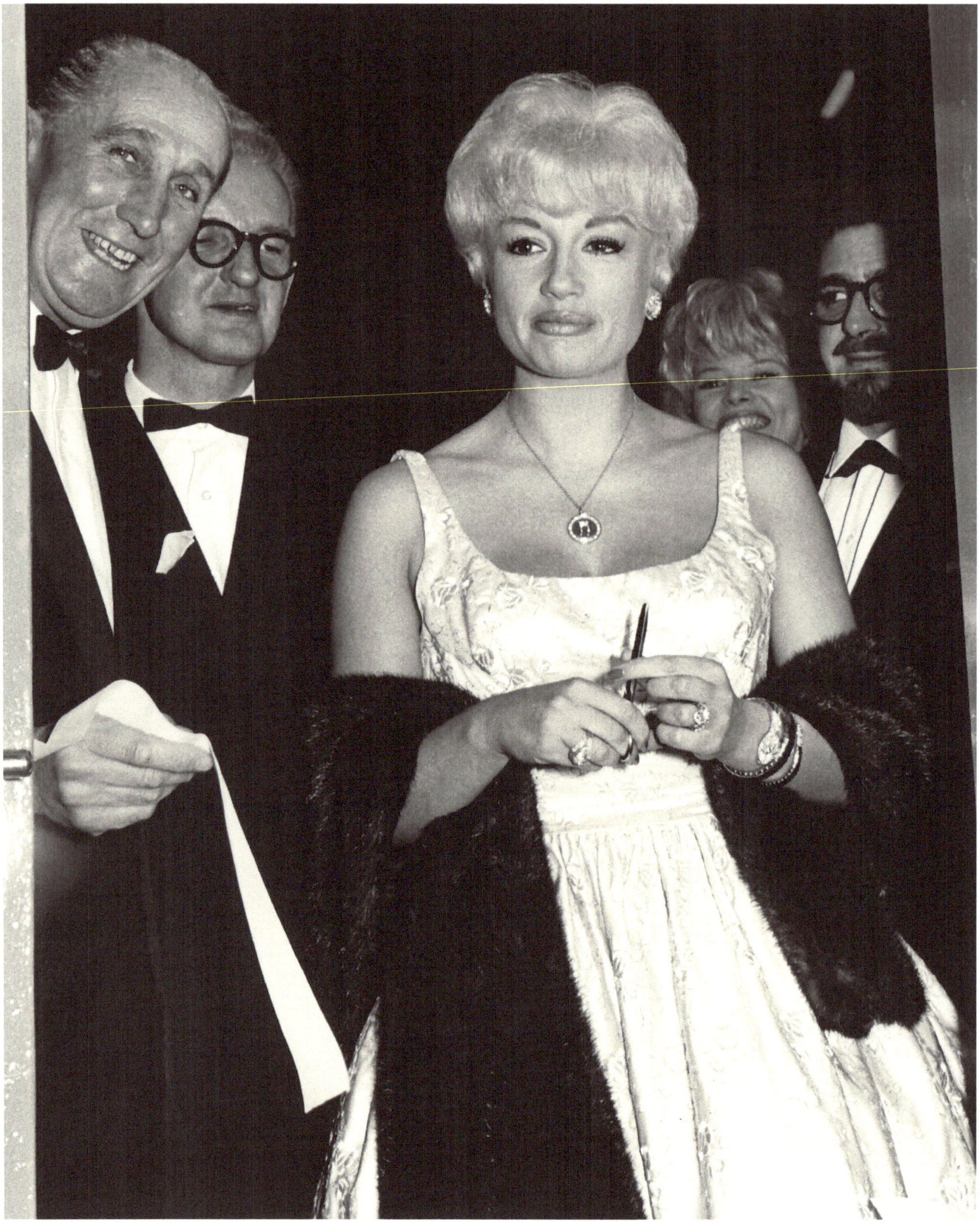

Endgame

Over the course of the filming the titled had changed to *As Nature Intended*, and later, at the suggestion of Michael Klinger, it became *Naked – As Nature Intended*. Working with Trevelyan and The British Board of Film Censors Compton didn't expect any further cuts as they submitted the film to the BBFC. Trevelyan, however, felt the film showed too much nudity and banned it outright. Most of the nudies at the time received an "A" certificate allowing them to secure a national release. To get round this Compton submitted the film to the Greater London Council. As a local licensing authority they had the right to accept or reject the BBFC's certificate, impose additional cuts, or grant their own certificate. They saw no difference in content to the host of other "naturist" movies that had been released in the capital and passed the film with few reservations.

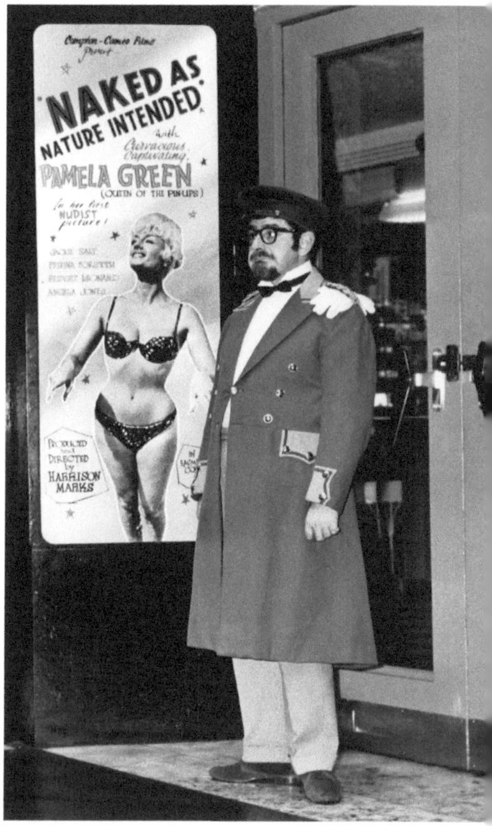

On the 30th November 1961 *Naked – As Nature Intended* received its world premiere as the debut feature of the newly refurbished Cameo-Moulin Cinema in Windmill Street. I was billed as the 'Queen of the Pin-ups' in her first nudist picture and Marks was christened 'King of the Camera'.

Twelve days earlier the Cameo had been running hour long cartoon programmes to casual attendances, but now in the street made famous by the Windmill

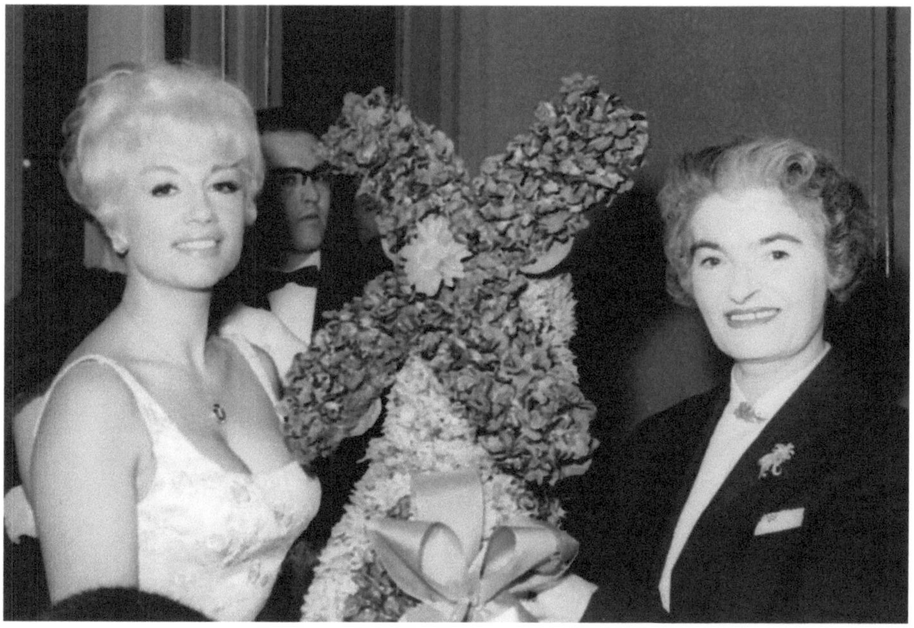

Above: Harrison Marks outside the Cameo-Moulin Cinema wishing he had read the small print in the contract.

Far Left: Pamela Green cutting the ribbon at the opening of the newly refurbished Cameo-Moulin Cinema in Windmill Street, at the world premiere of *Naked – As Nature Intended.*

Left: Miss Cousins, the long time cashier at the Cameo-Moulin presents Pamela, "Queen Of The Pin-ups", with a bouquet in the shape of a windmill.

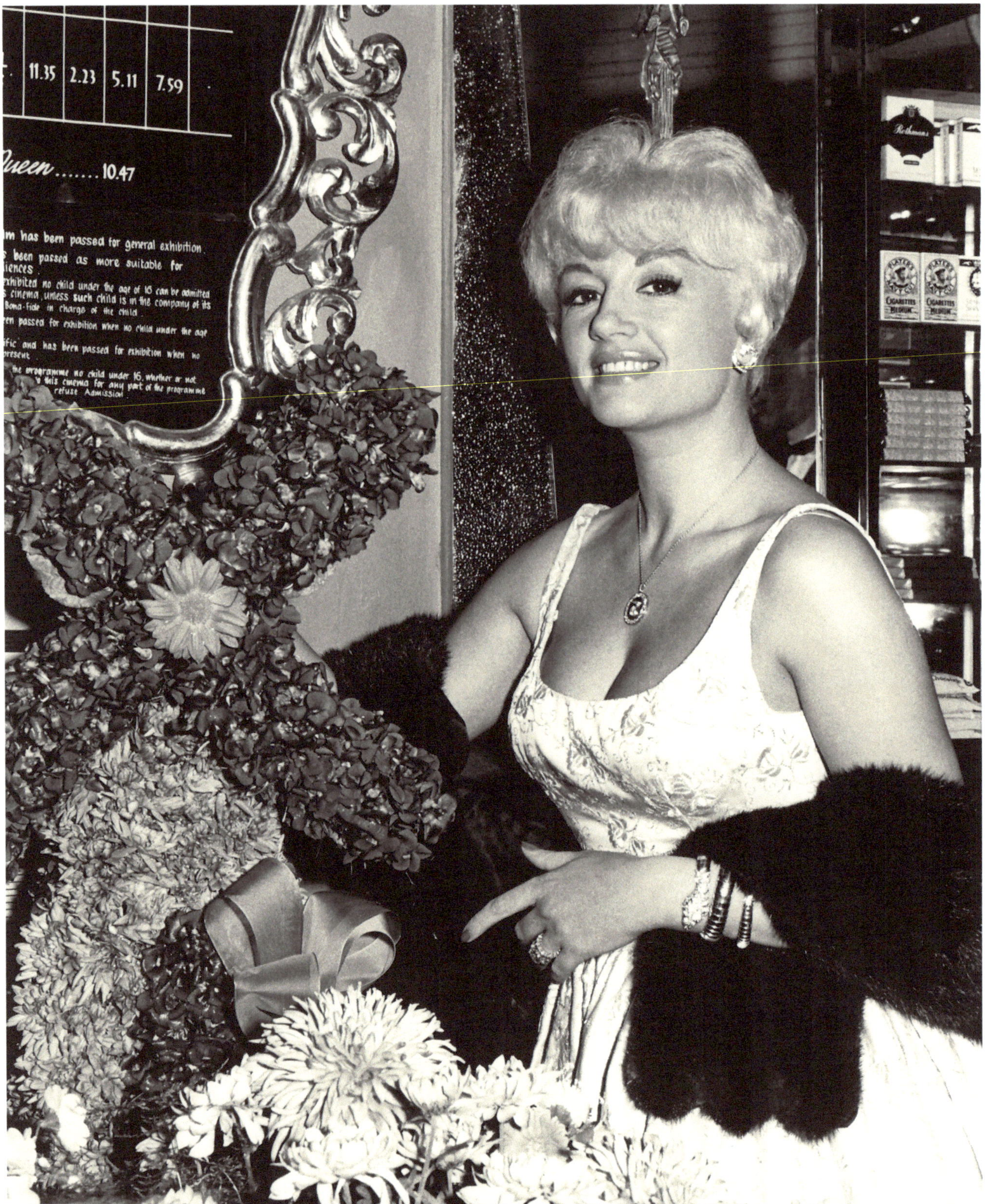
11.35 2.23 5.11 7.59
ueen.......10.47
has been passed for general exhibition.
been passed as more suitable for

Theatre, and where the unclothed feminine form catches the eye in club entrances, the Cameo-Moulin captured the queues on both sides of the street all the way down to Shaftesbury Avenue, even though it was pouring with rain.

All the cast along with the directors of the new distribution company, Compton-Cameo, were present.

I cut the inaugural ribbon and was presented with a rather large floral tribute in the shape of a windmill, by Miss Cousins, the head cashier who has been employed at the theatre for the last twenty-four years.

As the curtains drew back the light dimmed. There was the opening shot of me walking from the sea into camera, including my brief pause as I stepped into the pool and recovered my balance. Thankfully it was hardly noticeable. We watched in silence. It seemed to take forever before we finally got to the nude sequences. You should have the queues the next day. From eleven in the morning they were

Far left: Pamela Green in the Foyer of the Cameo- Moulin with the bouquet.

Below: Jackie, Pamela and Bridget at the premiere with George lurking in the background.

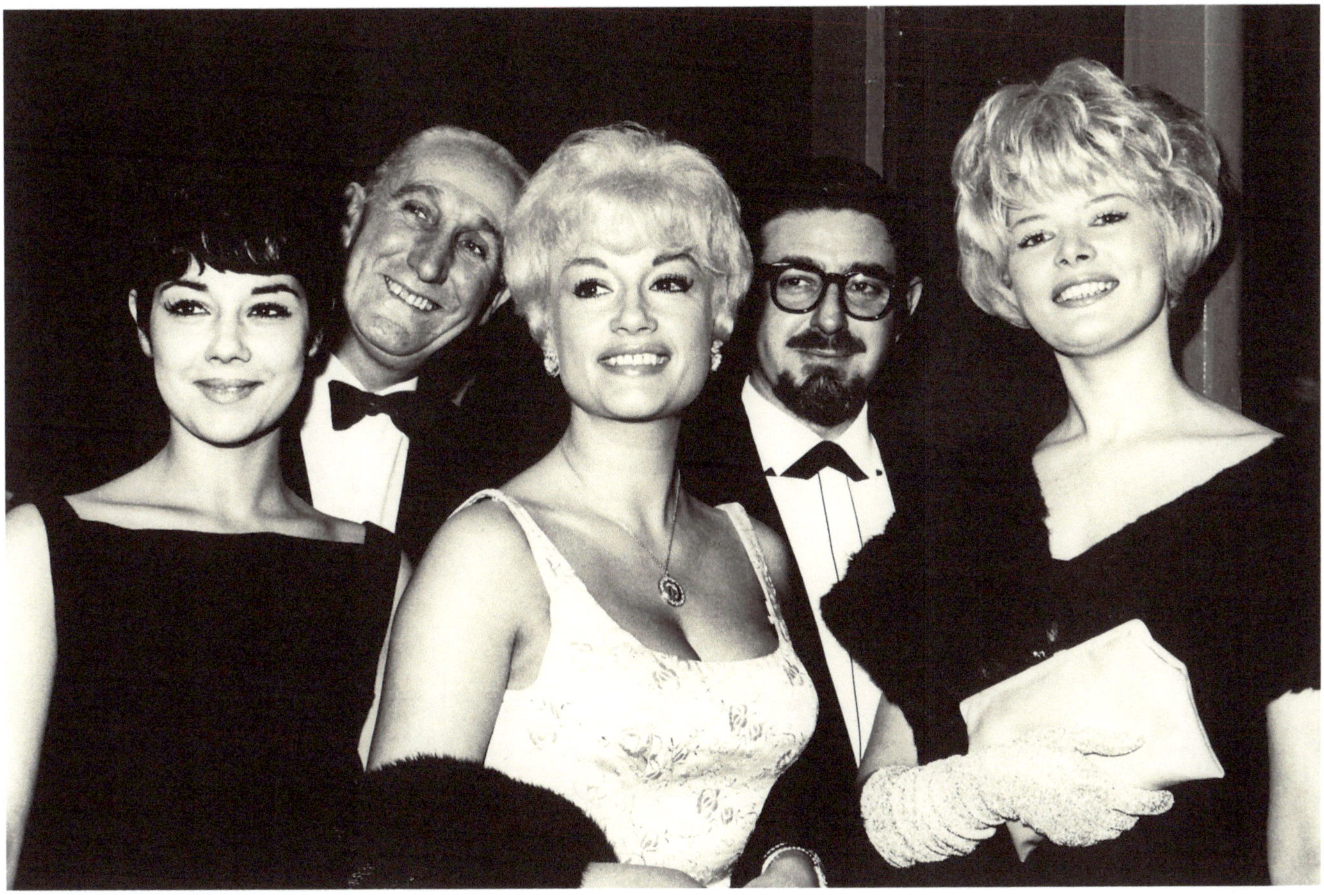

Below left: Newspaper advertising block.

Below right: UK film poster. Quad crown 30" x 40".

Right: Compton-Cameo press ad using a publicity photo of Pamela Green from the short-film *The Window Dresser* (1961).

besieging the theatre. When the film went on general release it was banned by Birmingham City Council. The cinema in neighbouring Walsall made a fortune. The independent distribution company Crown International picked up the film for release in North America.

As for the reviews, it was as badly received as any other nudist film. As David McGillivray wrote it was a lesson in suspense: "Not until twenty minutes from the end does Pamela realise that there is nothing wrong or improper or unnatural about nudity, and off comes the inhibiting bikini. A minute longer and less robust patrons may have needed medical aid."[1]

But that didn't stop the film from running for the next 18 months.

1 McGillivray, David, *Doing Rude Things*, Sun Tavern Fields, 1992.

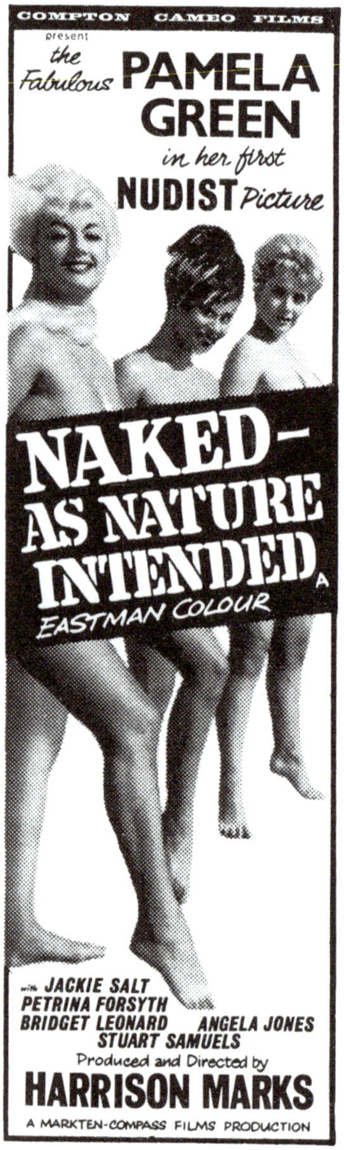

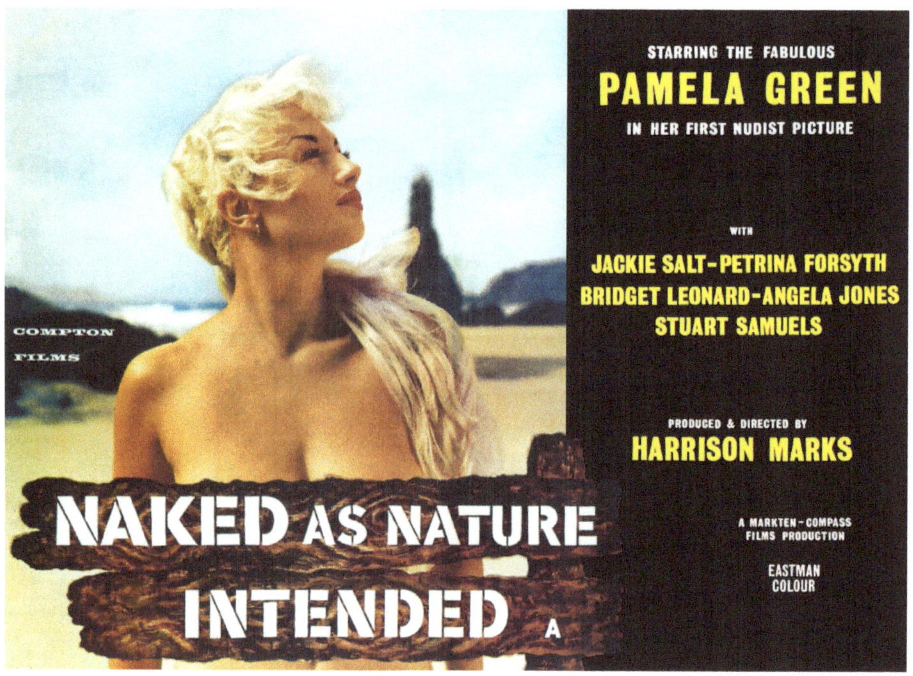

KINEMATOGRAPH WEEKLY
December 14, 1961

COMPTON-CAMEO FILMS LTD.

60-62 OLD COMPTON STREET, LONDON, W.1 Telephone: GERrard 1522 (5 lines)

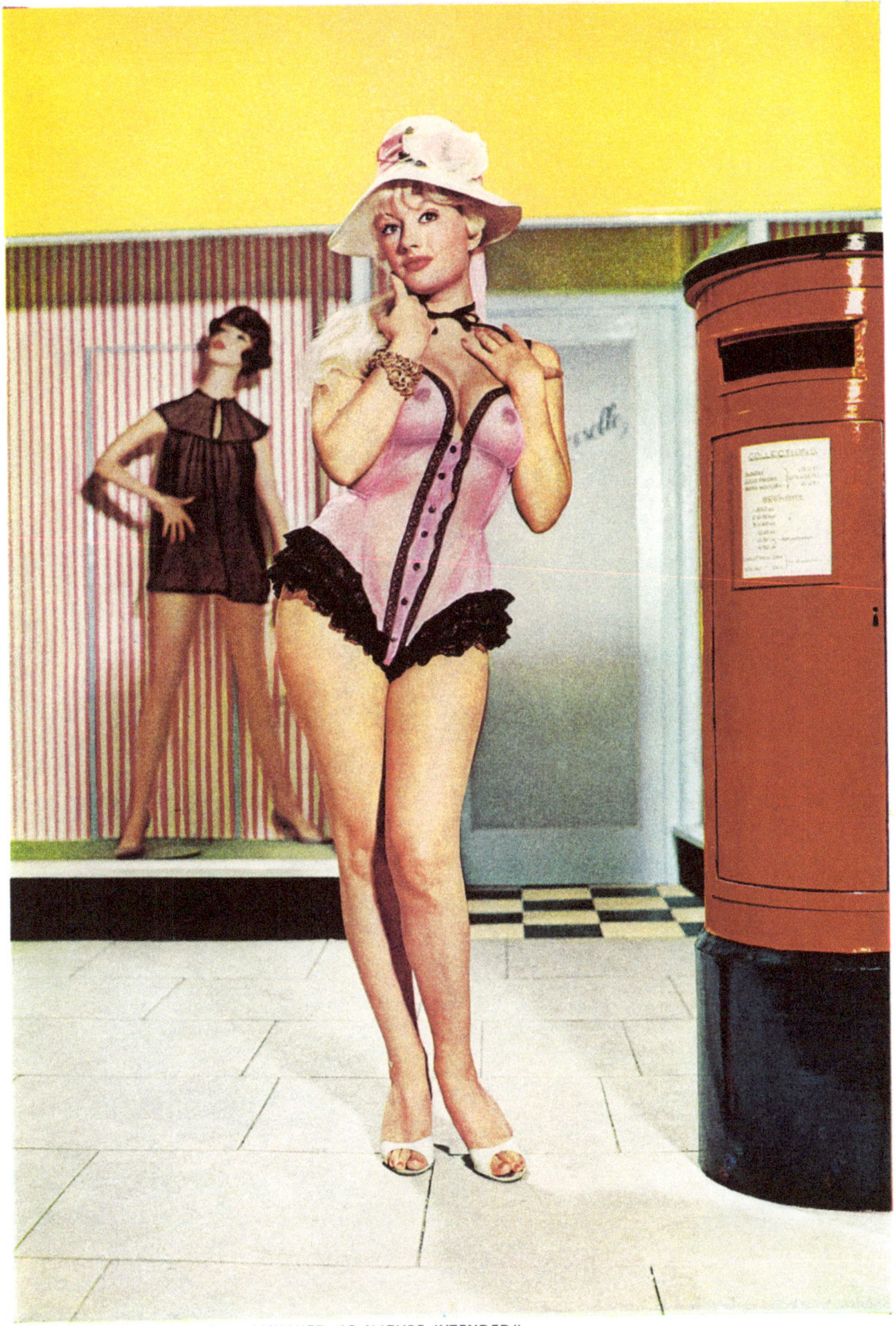

PAMELA GREEN — Lovely Star of "NAKED AS NATURE INTENDED"

RELEASES FOR 1962

PAMELA GREEN
stars in her first NUDIST film
NAKED AS NATURE INTENDED (A)
EASTMAN COLOUR
Produced and Directed by
HARRISON MARKS

BLONDE ANGELS . . .
FIERCE BRUNETTES . . . as
"Paris Playgirls" (X)
Directed by
BARBRO BOMAN

ANITA EKBERG
in
THE CALL GIRL BUSINESS (X)
with RENATO RASCEL

DANIELLE GAUBERT
in
PAVEMENTS OF PARIS (X)
Directed by
HENRI DECOIN

ALAIN RESNAIS'
Sensational Masterpiece
LAST YEAR IN MARIENBAD
VENICE FILM AWARD, 1961
A Sebricon Film

The **PAUL GRAETZ**
production of
A DAY OF SIN
(X)
with JEAN SOREL
(ENGLISH SPEAKING)
A Sebricon Film

ANOUK AIMEE · MARC MICHEL
in
"Lola" (X)
Written and Directed by
JACQUES DEMY
A Sebricon Film

PASCALE ROBERTS
in
'The DAMNED and the DARING' (A)
with PIERRE MONDY

COUNT ON COMPTON-CAMEO IN 1962

M.L.S.

Girls are seen leaving entrance, waving to "residents".

Camera pans with them to car.

. M.L.S. Girls, Car, Club Entrance. EXT. Evening.

The girls are seen putting luggage in car and climbing in.

3. M.L.S. Girls, Car, EXT. Evening.

The car is seen facing

turns full-lock on to

34. L.S. Car, Road,

Car travelling along

and holds on car as

sunset.

HOL

Shark-fishing se

and as available

HEREAF

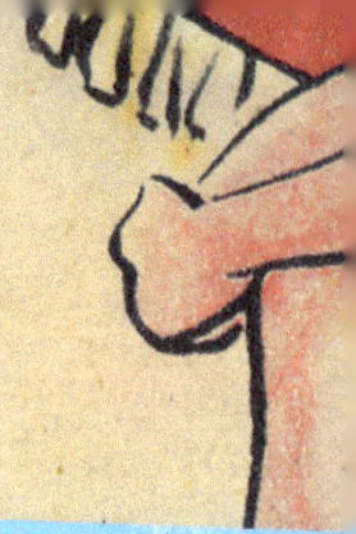

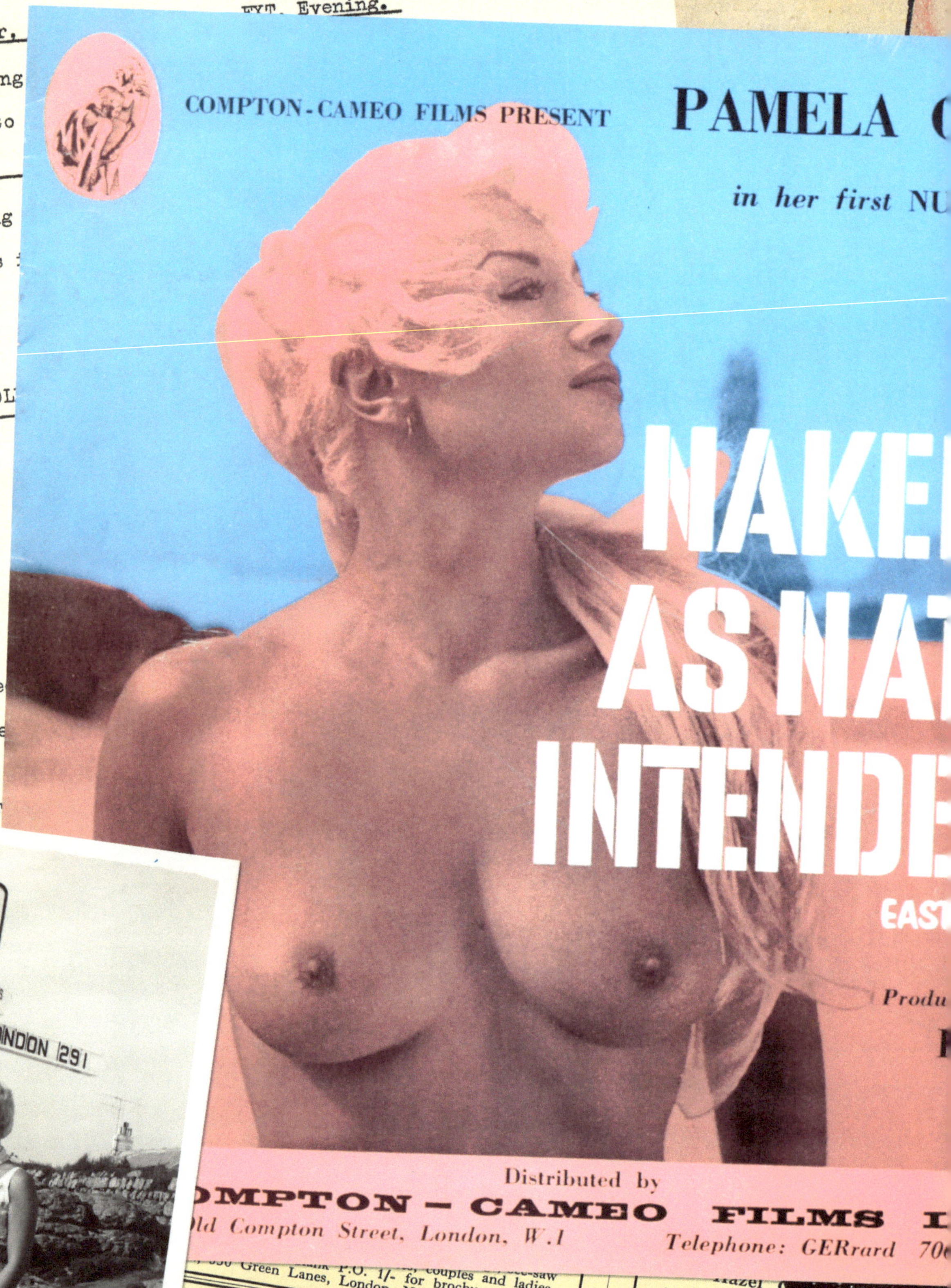

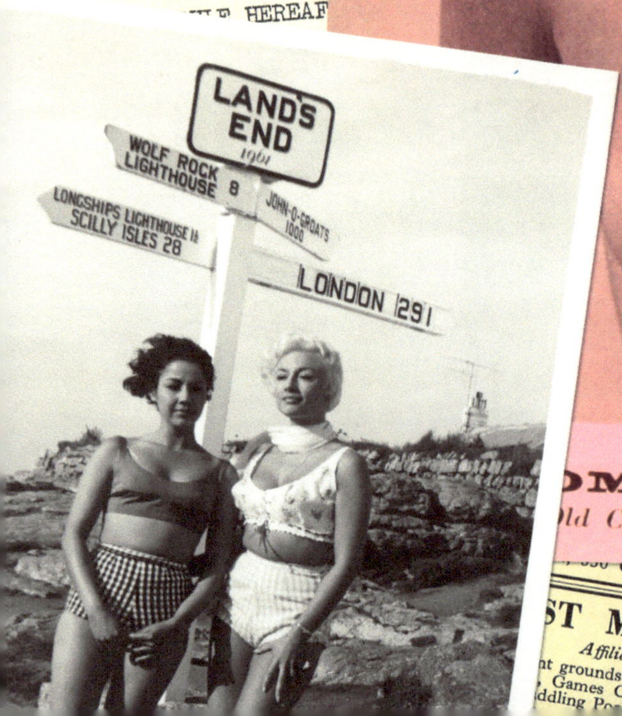

Green Lanes, London, N.4. P.O. 1/- for brochure to N/4, couples and ladies.

ST MIDLAND SUNFOLK

Affiliated to the B.S.B.A. and F.B.S.C.

nt grounds between Retford and Li

Games Courts, Pavili

A nudist club of well-equipped. M families.

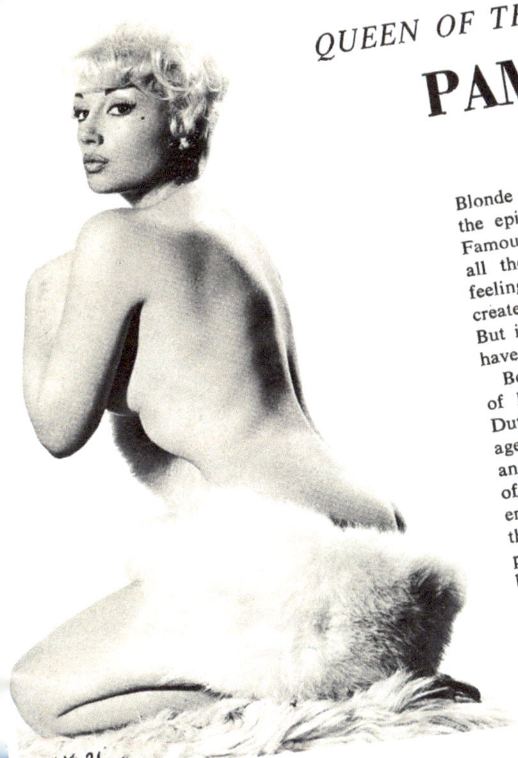

QUEEN OF THE PIN-UPS

PAMELA GREEN

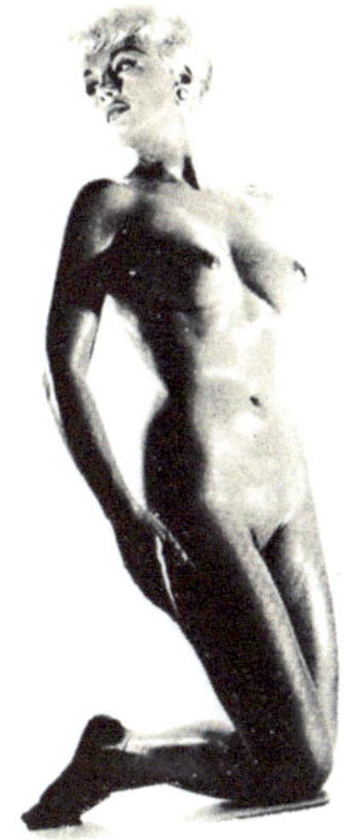

Blonde vivacious PAMELA GREEN has become the epitome of figure modelling the world over. Famous already in America, France, Japan and all the Scandinavian countries, her tremendous feeling for the classic line in modelling has created a fantastic reputation that is renowned. But it is interesting to note that her career could have taken more than one channel.

Born in Kingston-on-Thames, she spent most of her early years in Holland and thus speaks Dutch as fluently as she speaks English. At the age of seven Pamela commenced tuition in music and later entered an Academy with the thoughts of becoming a concert pianist. But at sixteen she enrolled in a London Art School and studied for three years which included one most successful period when one of her paintings was accepted by the Royal Academy.

At this time, however, the theatre fired her imagination, and after attending an audition for the Folies Bergere Pamela made a stage debut at the Prince of Wales theatre, London. It was during the run of this show that she met Harrison Marks, then a successful theatrical photographer who invited her to model for him. Thus one of the most prosperous partnerships of glamour photography in this country began and together they have produced some of the finest work in this branch of the profession ever seen.

In 1960 Michael Powell offered Pamela a starring role in 'PEEPING TOM', and her latest part prior to 'NAKED AS NATURE INTENDED' was in Val Guest's production of 'THE DAY THE EARTH CAUGHT FIRE'.

PAMELA GREEN stars in her first nudist role in 'NAKED AS NATURE INTENDED'.

KING OF THE CAMERA

HARRISON MARKS

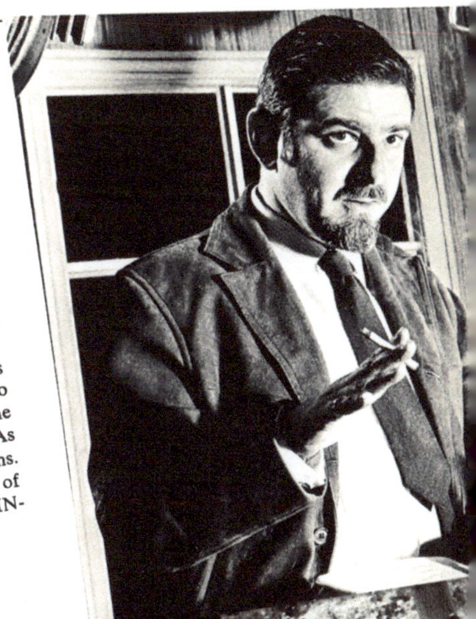

NAKED AS NATURE INTENDED, produced and directed by HARRISON MARKS vividly portrays on the screen the brilliant versatility of this outstanding artist with the camera.

Britain's most famous photographer on the portrayal of feminine beauty, his work now has a tremendous reputation in most countries throughout the world.

London born, where he still lives and operates his West End studios, the foundation of his career springs from the theatre where some of the greatest names in British and American show business posed for him.

His work shows a deep understanding of the beauty of women, and therefore when he was commissioned by a national magazine to photograph a well-known star, he produced his first international 'glamour magazine' shots. The impact proved terrific, and with a new well earned reputation, HARRISON MARKS decided to devote himself entirely to this branch of the profession.

In the past year, however, he has extended his sphere of activities by forming a company to produce short comedy films for children with the old slapstick touch but a modern outlook. As well as directing he has appeared in several films.

Now the cinema screen reflects the artistry of this craftsman in NAKED AS NATURE INTENDED.

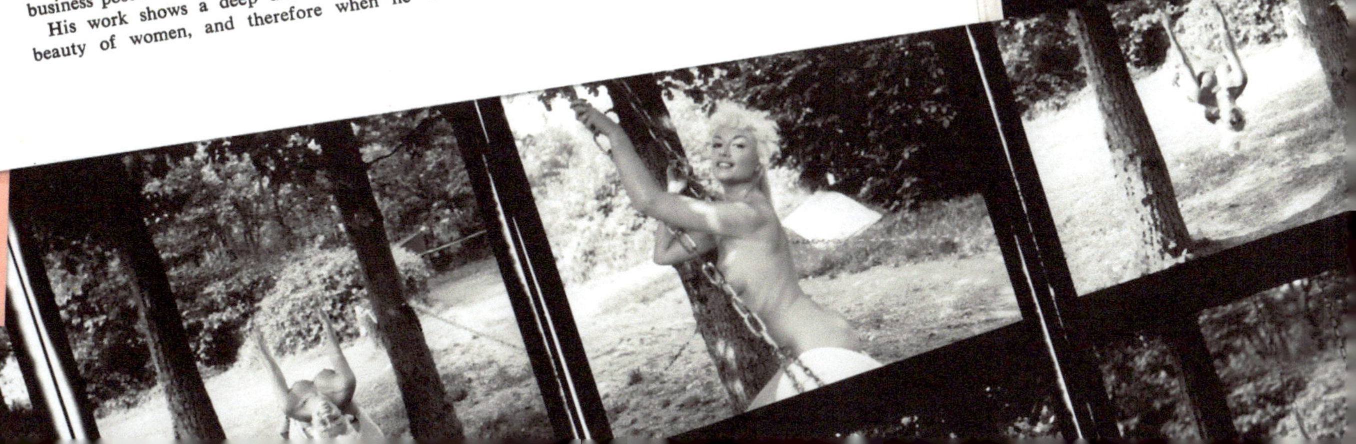

AVAILABLE TITLES FROM WOLFBAIT

Doing Rude Things
The history of the British sex film.

NEW! **Cinema au Naturel**
A history of nudist film.

Miniten: Rules of the Game
Invented in the 1930s, Miniten is a tennis-like game played by naturists.

Naked as Nature Intended
The epic tale of a nudist picture by Pamela Green, with photographs by Douglas "Dambuster" Webb, DFM.

The Naked Truth About Harrison Marks
The notorious biography by Franklyn Wood.

Past Masters of the Nude
An illustrated bibliography of nude photography books published in England from 1896 to 1960.

THE STEPHEN GLASS COLLECTION

Amazons of Yesteryear
A rare, action-packed collection of images of wrestling women of the 1940s and 1950s.

Beauty Off-Duty
Relaxed, everyday moments caught on camera.

Naked in the Menagerie
A playful look at Eve accompanied by her animal friends.

Nudist Camp Follies – volumes 1 and 2
An intimate look at the natural and free atmosphere in Sun Clubs.

Nymphs and Naiads
Beauty unadorned and outdoors.

NEW! **Poise and Pose**
A magnificent series of photographs of female beauty taken in the studio.

Order online at wolfbait.co.uk

www.ingramcontent.com/pod-product-compliance
Ingram Content Group UK Ltd.
Pitfield, Milton Keynes, MK11 3LW, UK
UKHW061033310726
14089UKWH00010B/229
* 9 7 8 0 9 5 4 5 9 8 5 9 4 *

AMAZONS OF YESTERYEAR ★★★★

WRESTLING WOMEN OF THE 1940S AND '50S

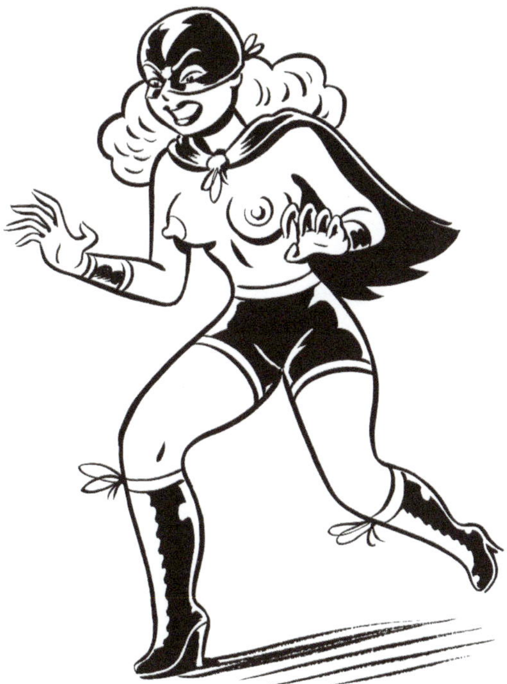

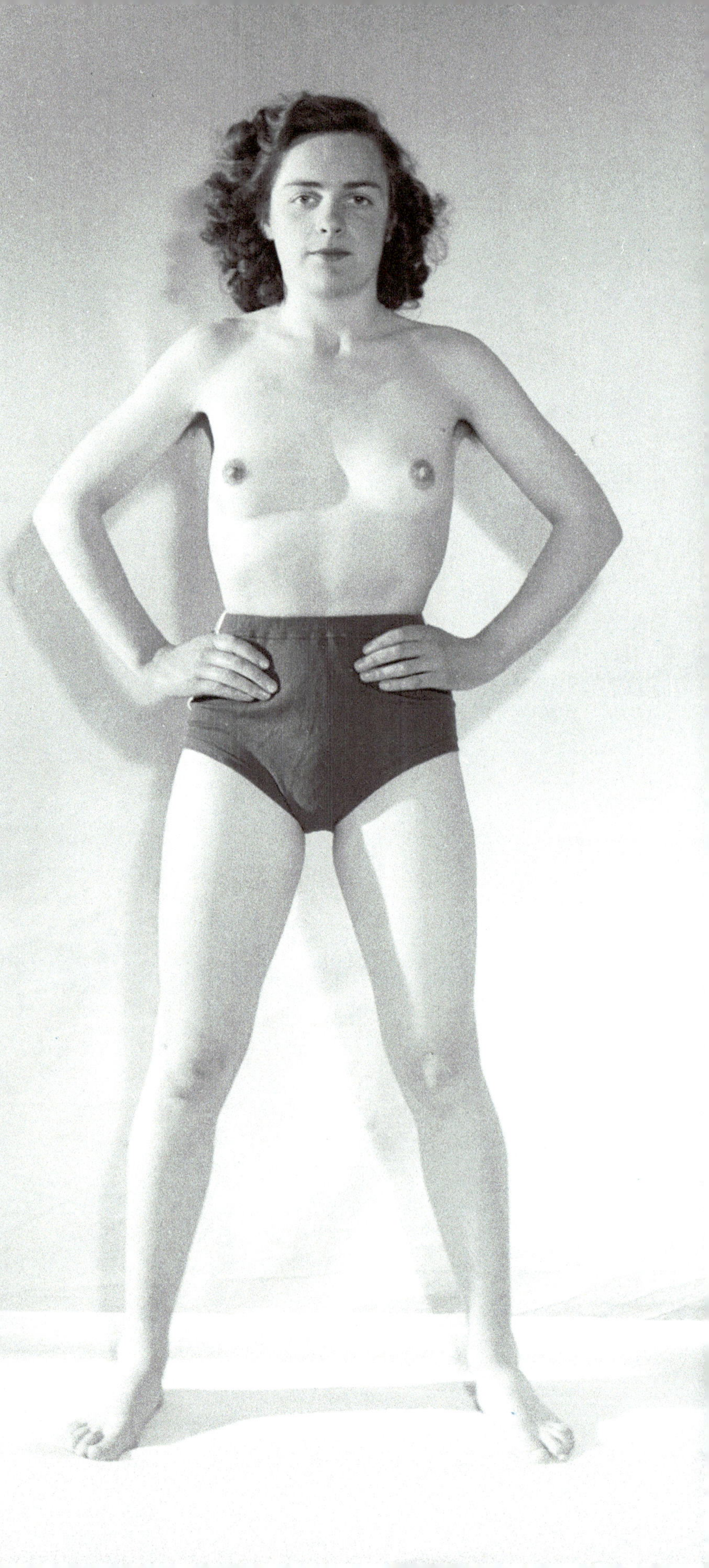

Published in 2017 by Wolfbait Books © 2017

ISBN 978-1-9997441-1-3 (hardback)

A catalogue record of this book is available at The British Library.

AMAZONS OF YESTERYEAR ★★★★

WRESTLING WOMEN OF THE 1940S AND '50S

By Yahya El-Droubie

Photography by Stephen Glass

Illustrations by Colin Gordon

WOLFBAIT
UNDER THE COUNTER CULTURE

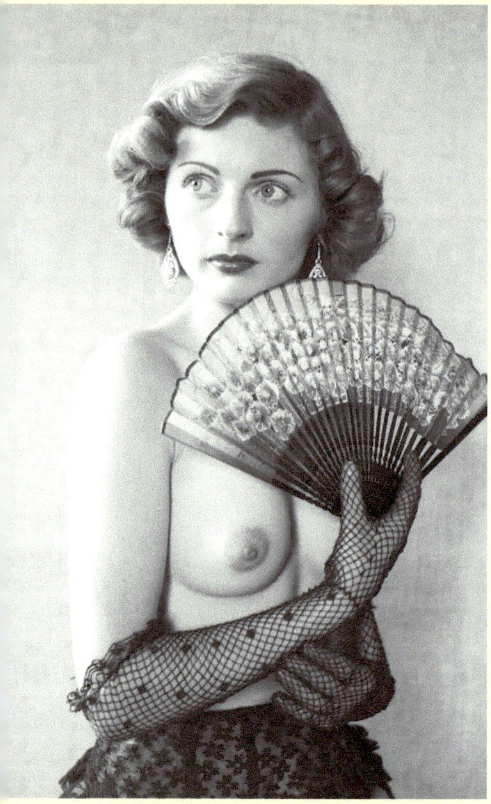

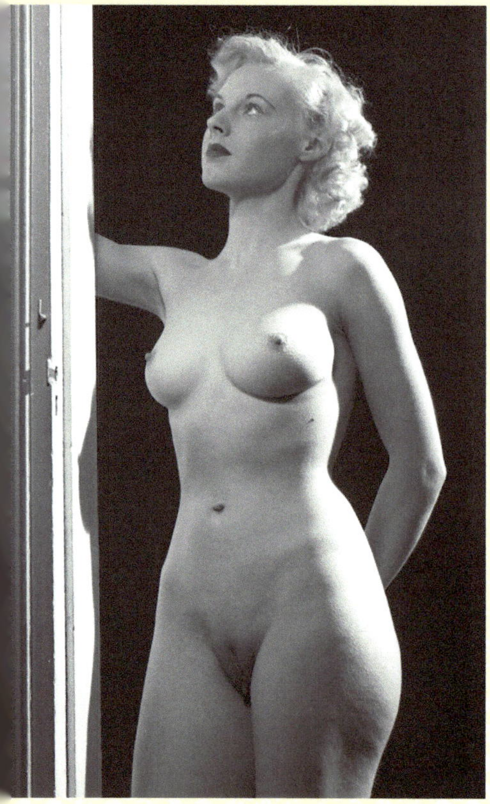

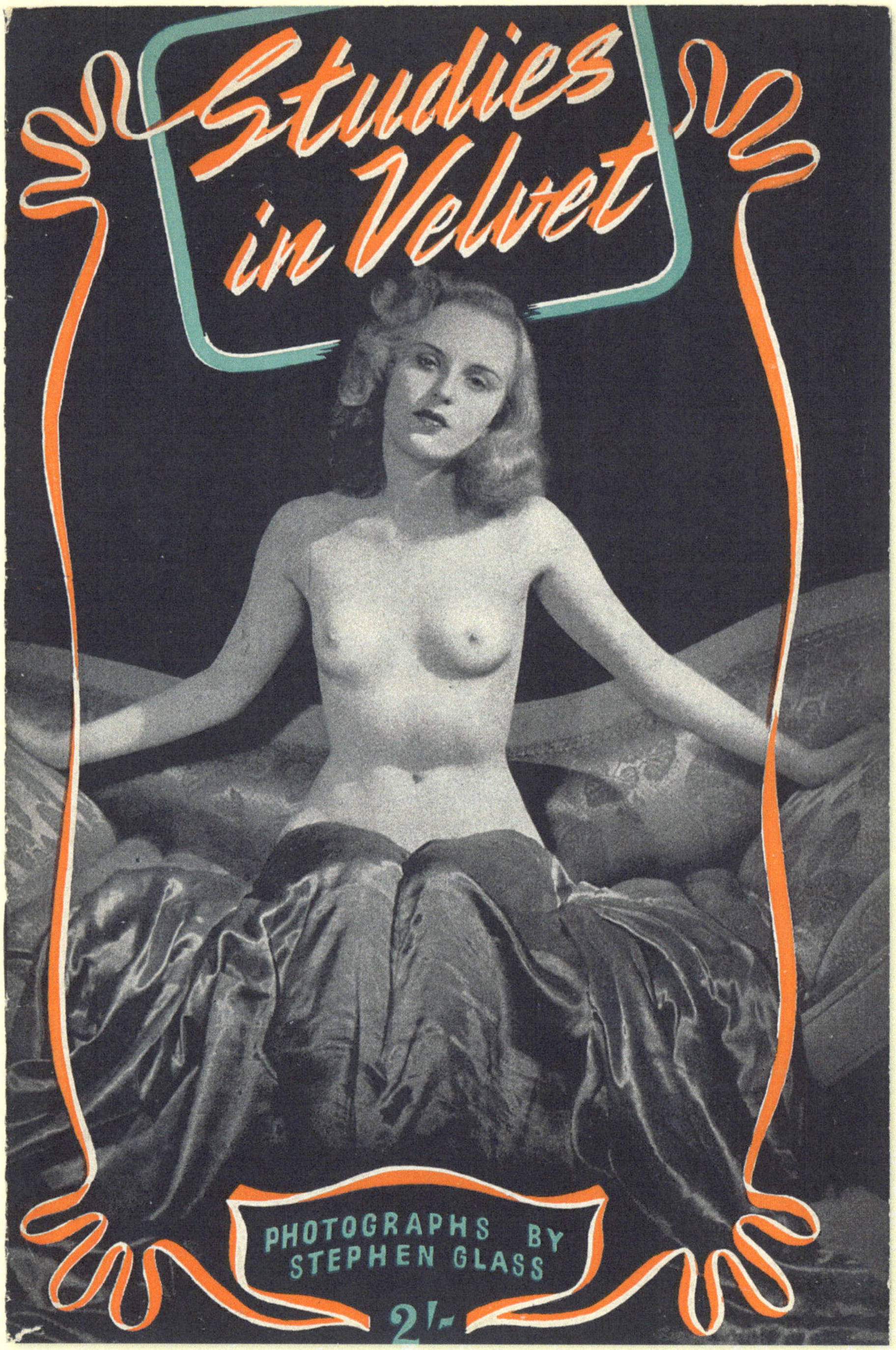

Above: *Studies in Velvet, photographs by Stephen Glass*, Gnome Publications, Bedfordbury, Covent Garden. No date but probably late 1940s / early 1950s.

Left top: Studio nude probably taken in the late 1940s / early 1950s. Model unknown.
Left bottom: Studio nude probably taken in the late 1940s / early 1950s. Model unknown.

Introduction

THE PHOTOGRAPHER STEPHEN GLASS is a bit of an enigma. He was well-known enough during the 1950s for his name to be prominently displayed on the front of magazines to help sell them, but very little actually was written about him or his work.

This situation differs somewhat from that of his elder brother, Zoltán Glass, who was also a photographer. Known to his friends as "Zolly" he was featured and interviewed in numerous magazines on both sides of the Atlantic.

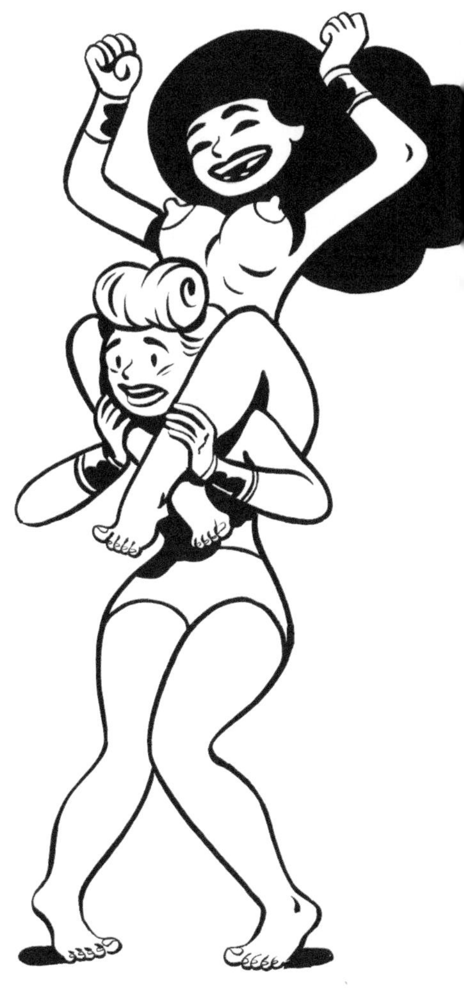

Zoltán was born in Budapest on April 26, 1903. He began his career as a cartoonist and retoucher for a local newspaper, but in 1925 he moved to Berlin, where he found regular employment as the picture editor of a Berlin evening paper, before moving on to the *Berliner Tagblatt* as a photojournalist. He prospered and was soon able to develop a thriving freelance business as a commercial photographer and journalist. He established Reclaphot, a photographic agency that specialised in advertising work, and Autophot, a company dedicated exclusively to automobile photography. He was an amateur racer and keen motorsport enthusiast, and he covered Germany's biggest races at the Nurburgring and the Avus circuit, near Berlin. His most famous photos are of the Mercedes-Benz Silver Arrows team, which dominated Grand Prix racing in the mid-1930s. With the rise of Hitler, however, business became increasingly difficult, and he fled to London. As an enemy alien at the outbreak of World War II, he was not permitted to pursue his profession and faced the threat of internment, so he voluntarily handed over his camera equipment to the British authorities.

After the war, he eked out a living taking publicity stills for clients in the film and theatrical worlds. His career took a big step up when the Hungarian Arpad Elfer who was Creative Director of Colman, Prentis & Varley, one of the most prestigious London ad agencies started giving him work. By the mid-Fifties, he was one of the most successful fashion and advertising photographers in London

A few years ago the idea of a girl in 'shorts' for running was enough to make Grandma gasp, but these Eves believe a 'bout' a day keeps the Doctor away.

with his own studios at 183 Kings Road, Chelsea, and later at 41 Paradise Walk, SW3. One of his clients was Odhams Press who published *Lilliput*, a pocket-sized gentleman's magazine that featured an assortment of titillating articles and risqué humour, together with adventurous photographic essays from such well-known talents as Bill Brandt and Brassai.

His brother Stephen, who also fled Europe due to the Second World War, carved out a name for himself taking pictures for such publications as *The Naturist* and *Health and Efficiency.*

The well-known Pamela Green (1929-2010) modelled for him several times at the infamous nudist camp Spielplatz in Bricket Wood and at his tiny first-floor studio in Old Church Street, just of the Kings Road in Chelsea. *"In those days, when Stephen photographed me, I still had dark hair. He liked his props, especially stuffed animals."* It was Pamela's agent Pearl Beresford, who sent her along to his brother, Zoltán, whose studio on the Kings Road was enormous by comparison. Unlike Stephen, Zoltán was brisk and businesslike.

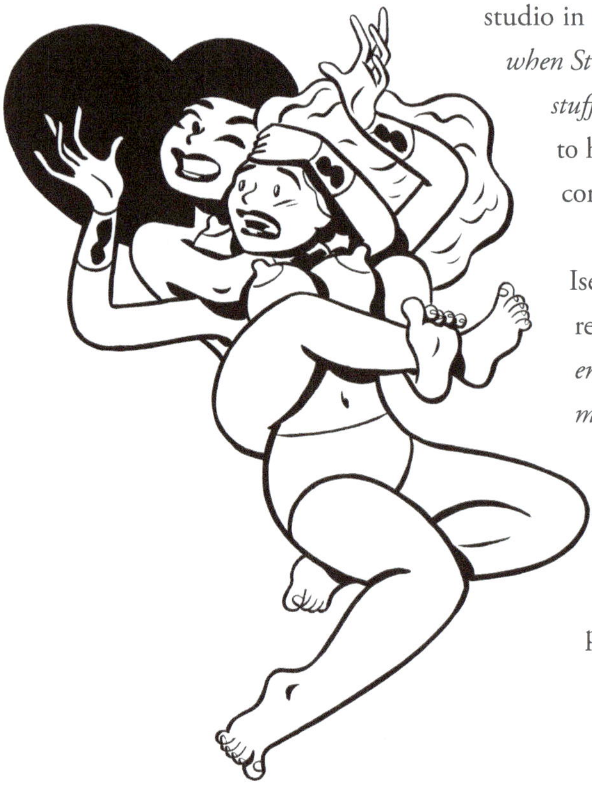

Iseult, the daughter of Charles Macaskie, the founder of Spielplatz, remembers Stephen. *"He would often ask me to pose for him. I quite enjoyed having my photo taken, but when I asked to be paid he stopped using me. A bit of pocket money back then would have been nice."*

In addition to magazines, his work graced a series of small books published by *The Naturist* such as *Sussex Maidens* (1949), *Pool of Enchantment* (1950) and *Nudist Life in Spielplatz* (1956). He also photographed the popular model June Palmer (1940-2004).

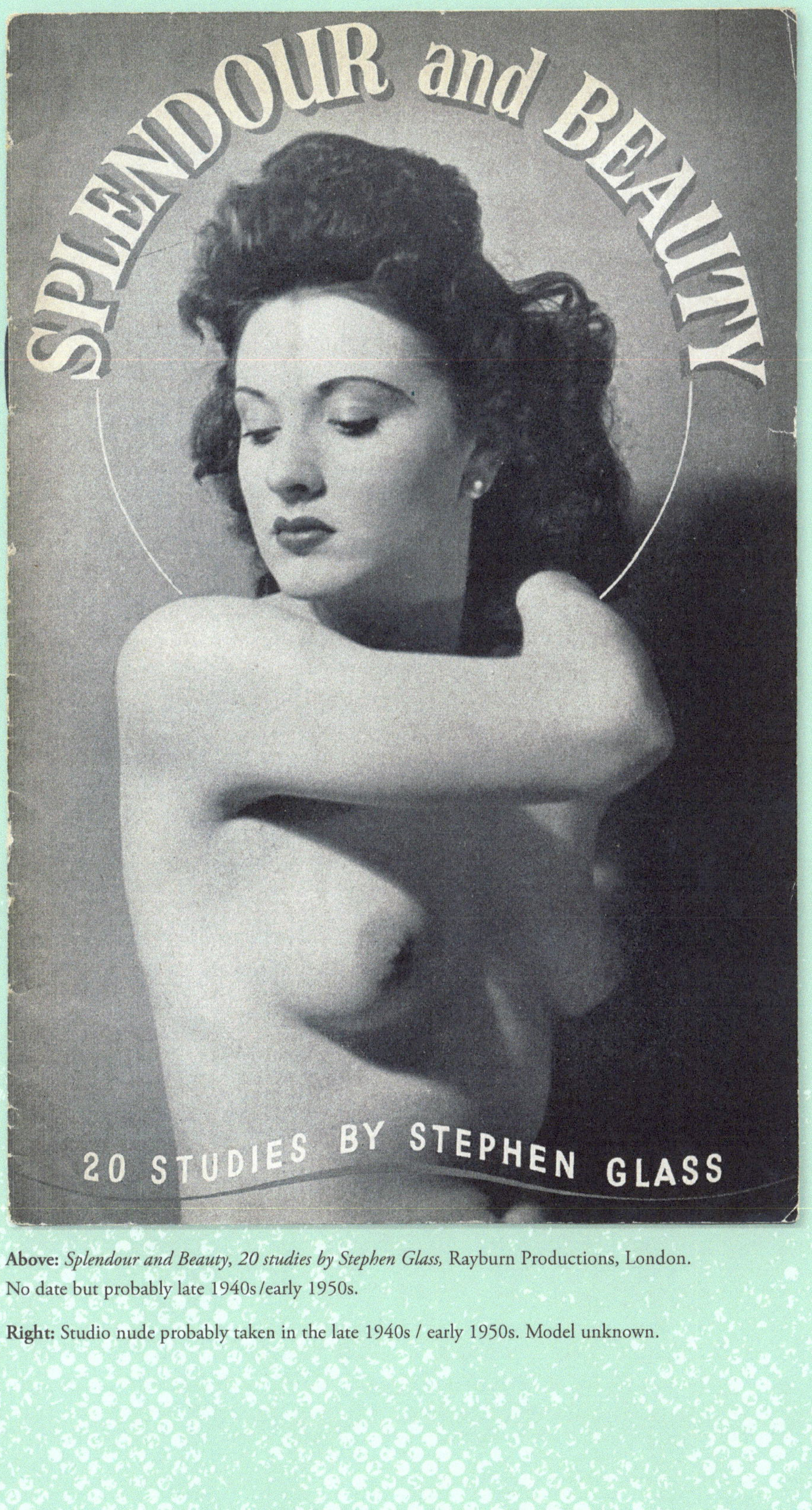

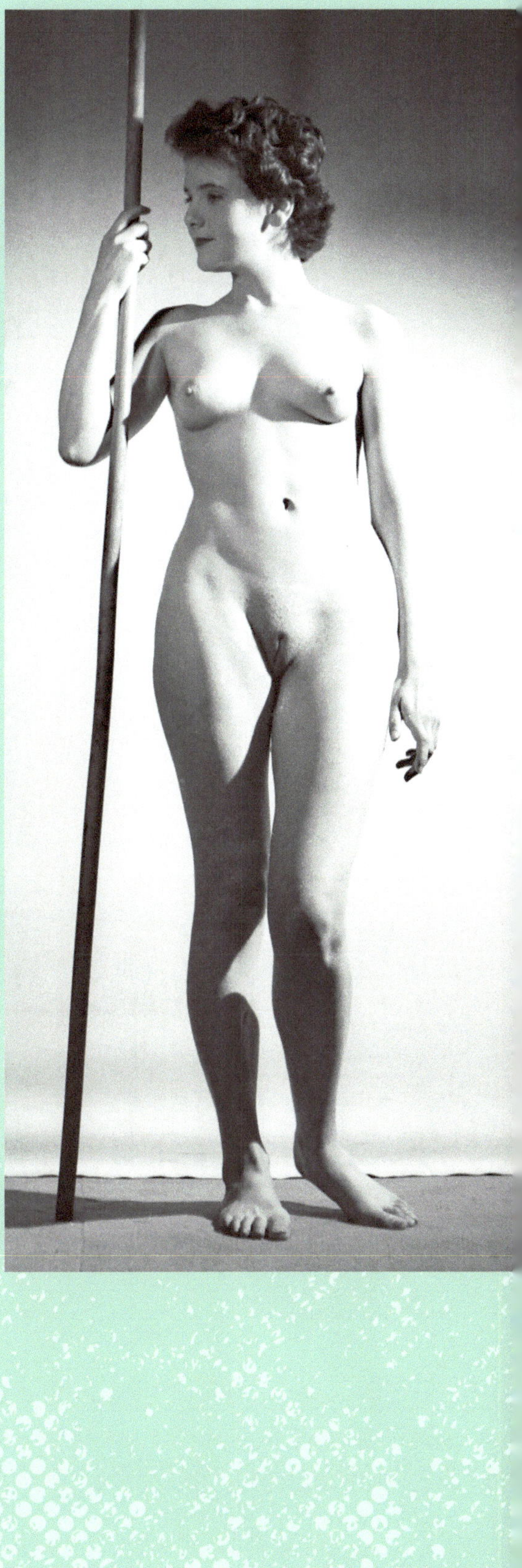

Above: *Splendour and Beauty, 20 studies by Stephen Glass,* Rayburn Productions, London. No date but probably late 1940s/early 1950s.

Right: Studio nude probably taken in the late 1940s / early 1950s. Model unknown.

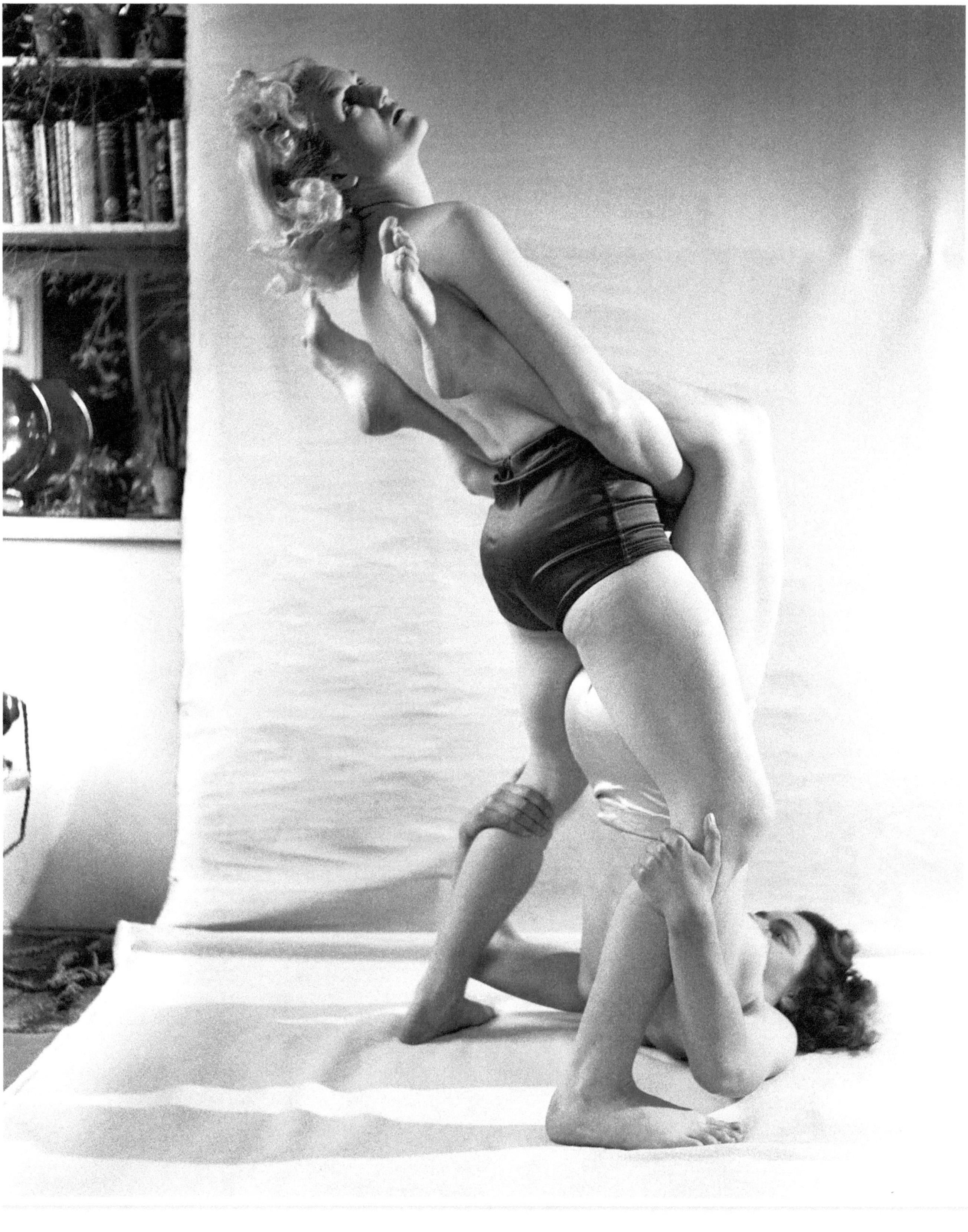

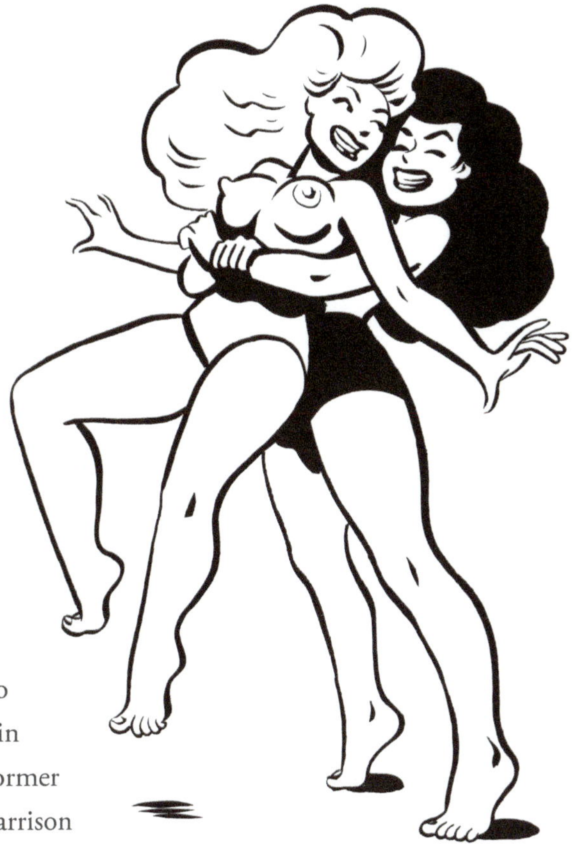

The photos in this book are from the uncensored negatives. Up and until the end of the 1960s the showing of pubic hair or genitalia was considered obscene in Britain. To ensure a photograph of a naked young lady was suitable for publication and did not incur the wrath of the censor, a model would shave down below, and the image would be retouched by hand to erase anything problematic.

In 1964 Zoltán Glass had made enough money to sell his Chelsea studio to a consortium of British photographers and move abroad to a villa in Roquebrune on the French Riviera with his common-law wife Pat, a former cabaret dancer. He offered his collection of pin-up photography to Harrison Marks, who strangely turned him down. He died in France on February 24, 1981, at the age of 78, leaving neither offspring nor a will. His photographs were eventually left to the The National Science and Media Museum in Bradford. Stephen Glass died on 23 April 1990. His work ended up at auction.

I have never seen the photos in this book published before now. The models seem to be amateurs and not professional wrestlers, but they do seem to be enjoying themselves. They were probably taken in Stephen's flat at 60 Old Church Street, less than a ten-minute walk from his brother's studio on the Kings Road. Occasionally Stephen would write on the back of the contact sheet or the negative bag, but all I can make out is the date 1947 and the names Margaret and Doris – may they live long in our memories. So sit back and satisfy your passions for female combat and nostalgia with this collection of rarely seen photos of bare-breasted wrestling women.

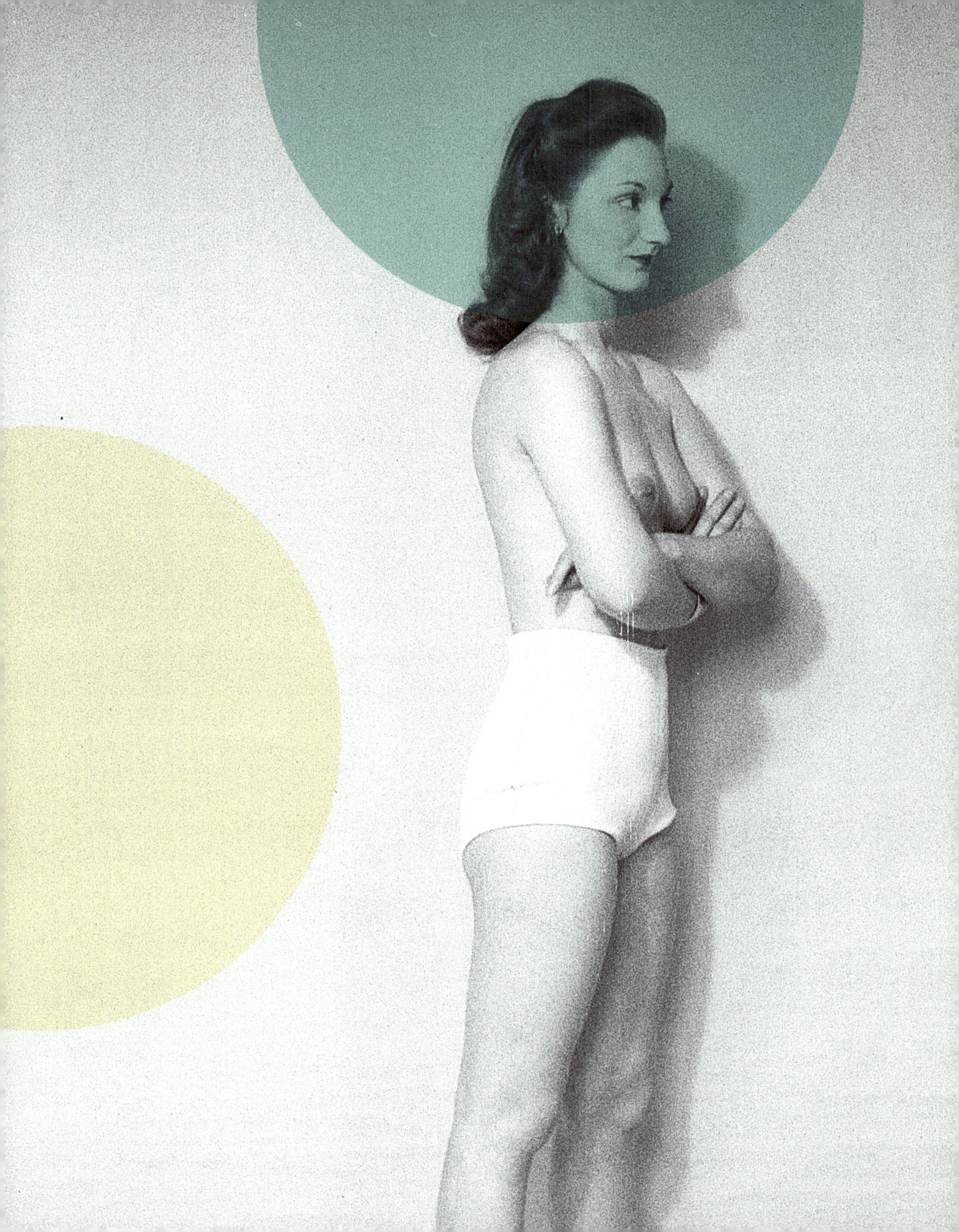

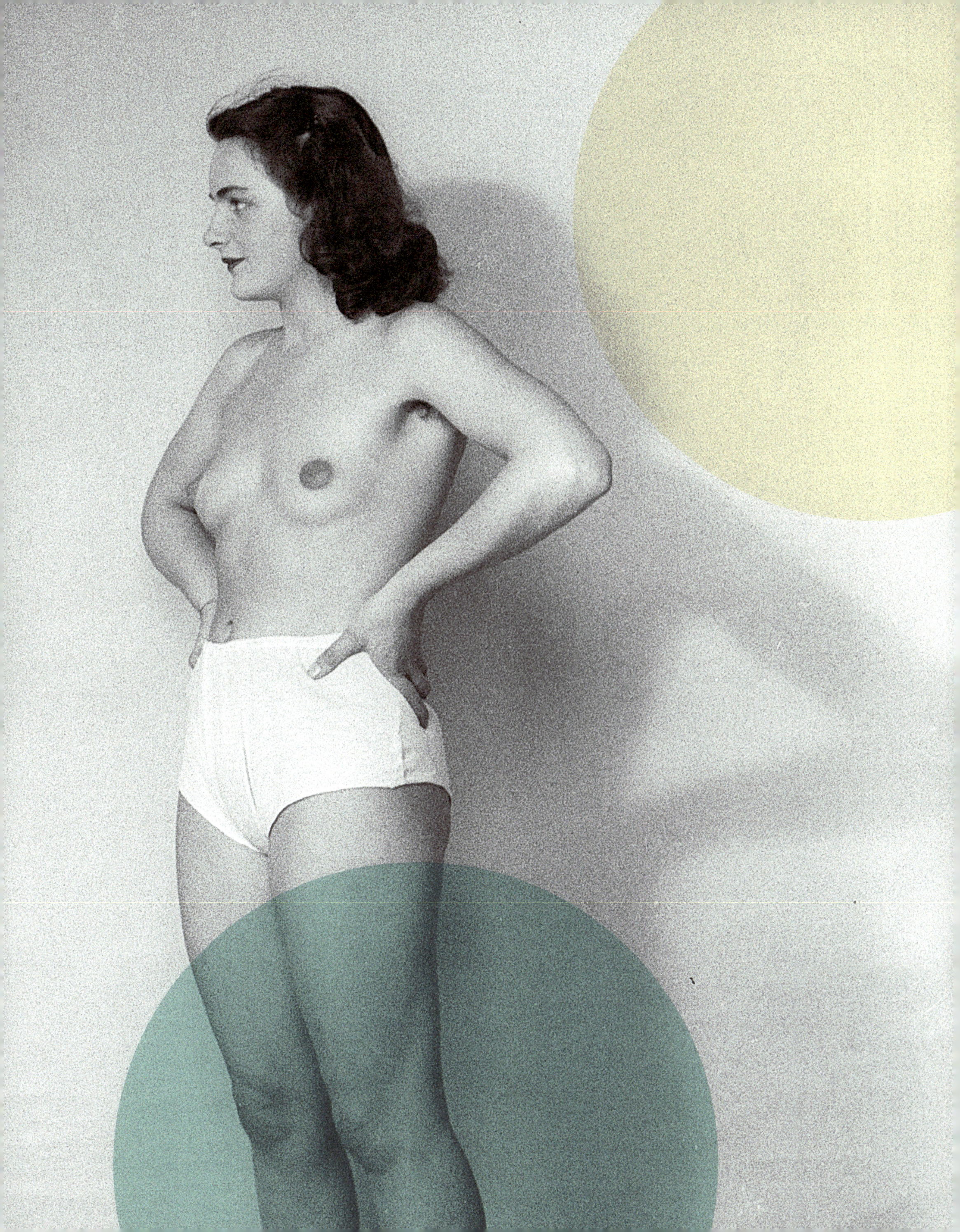

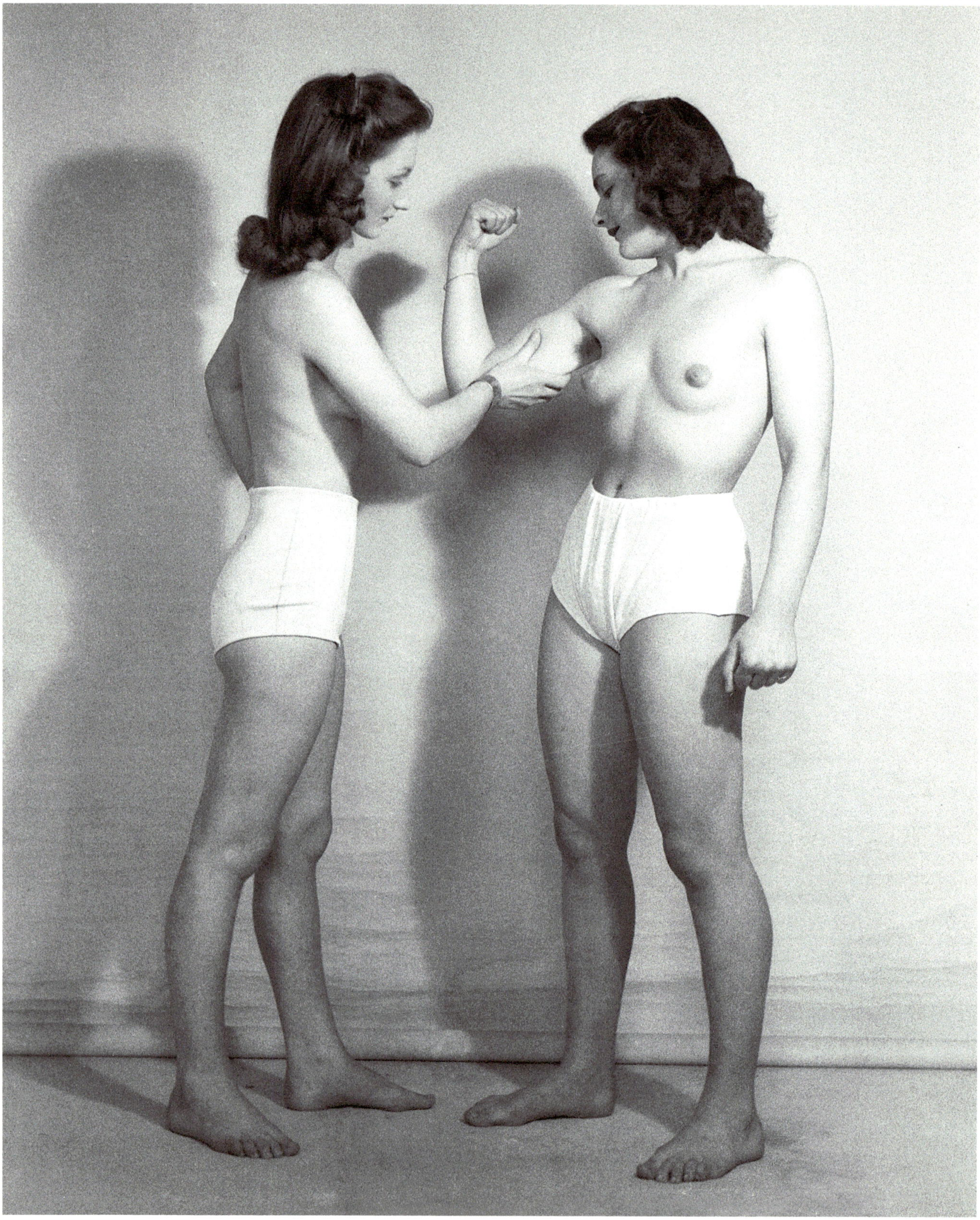

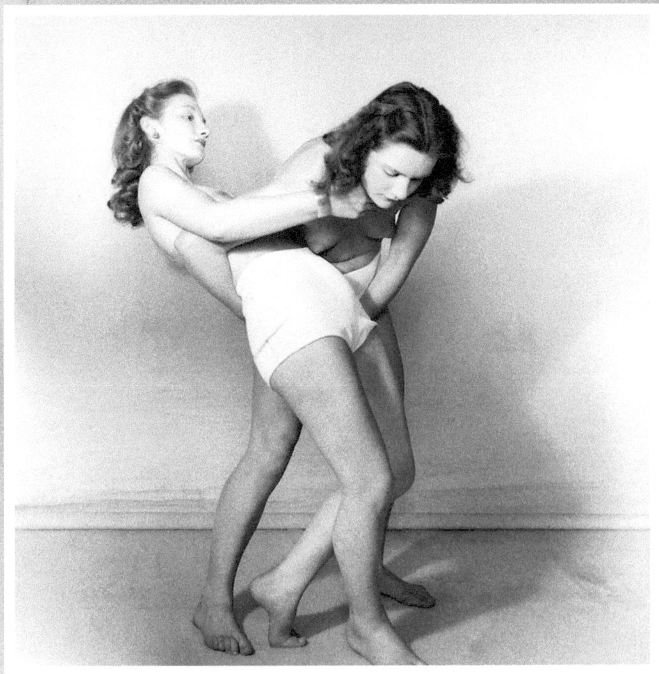
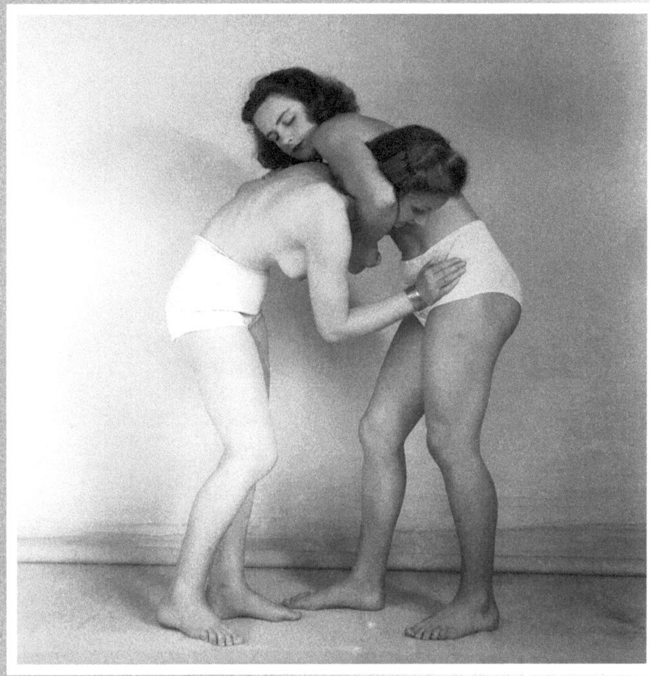
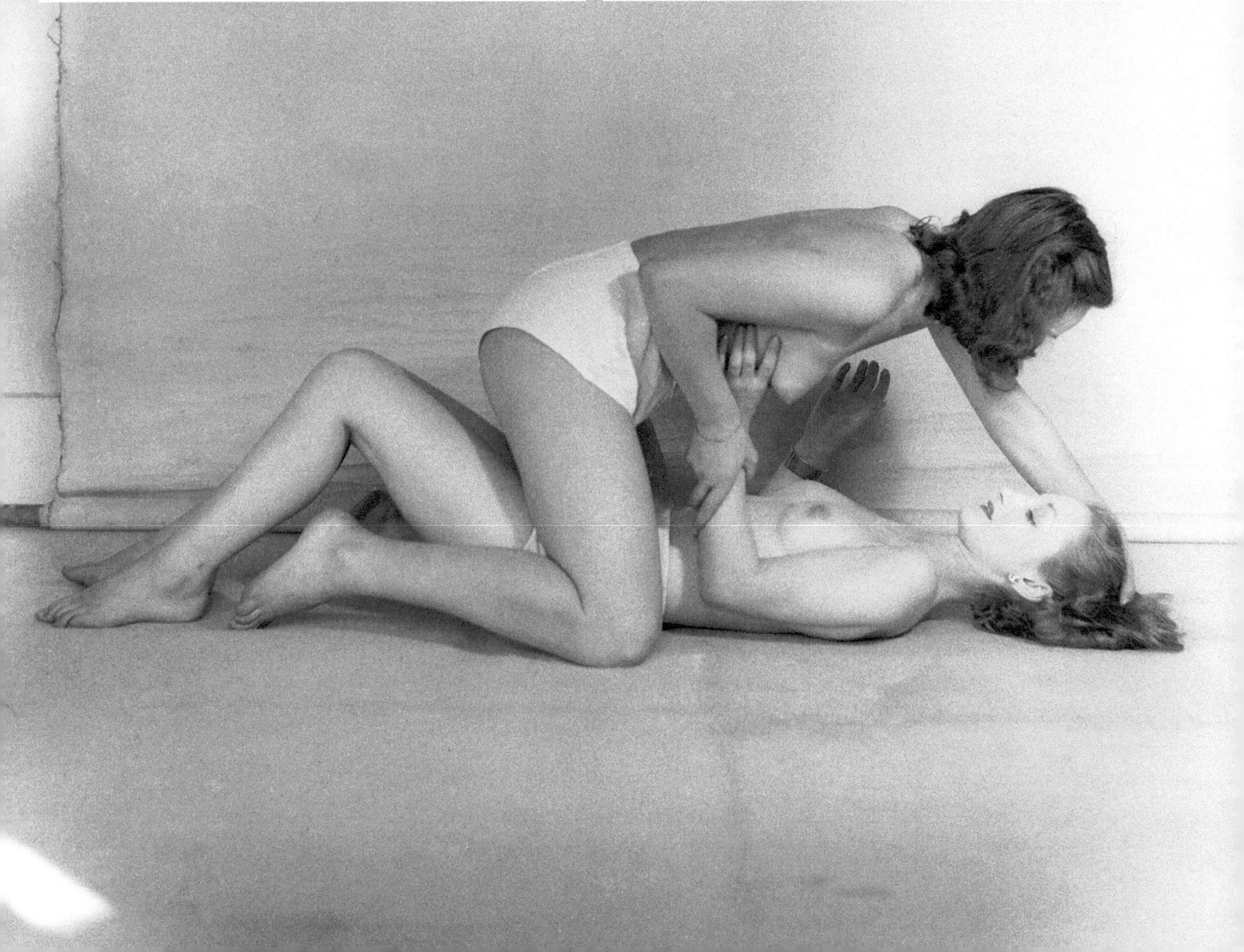

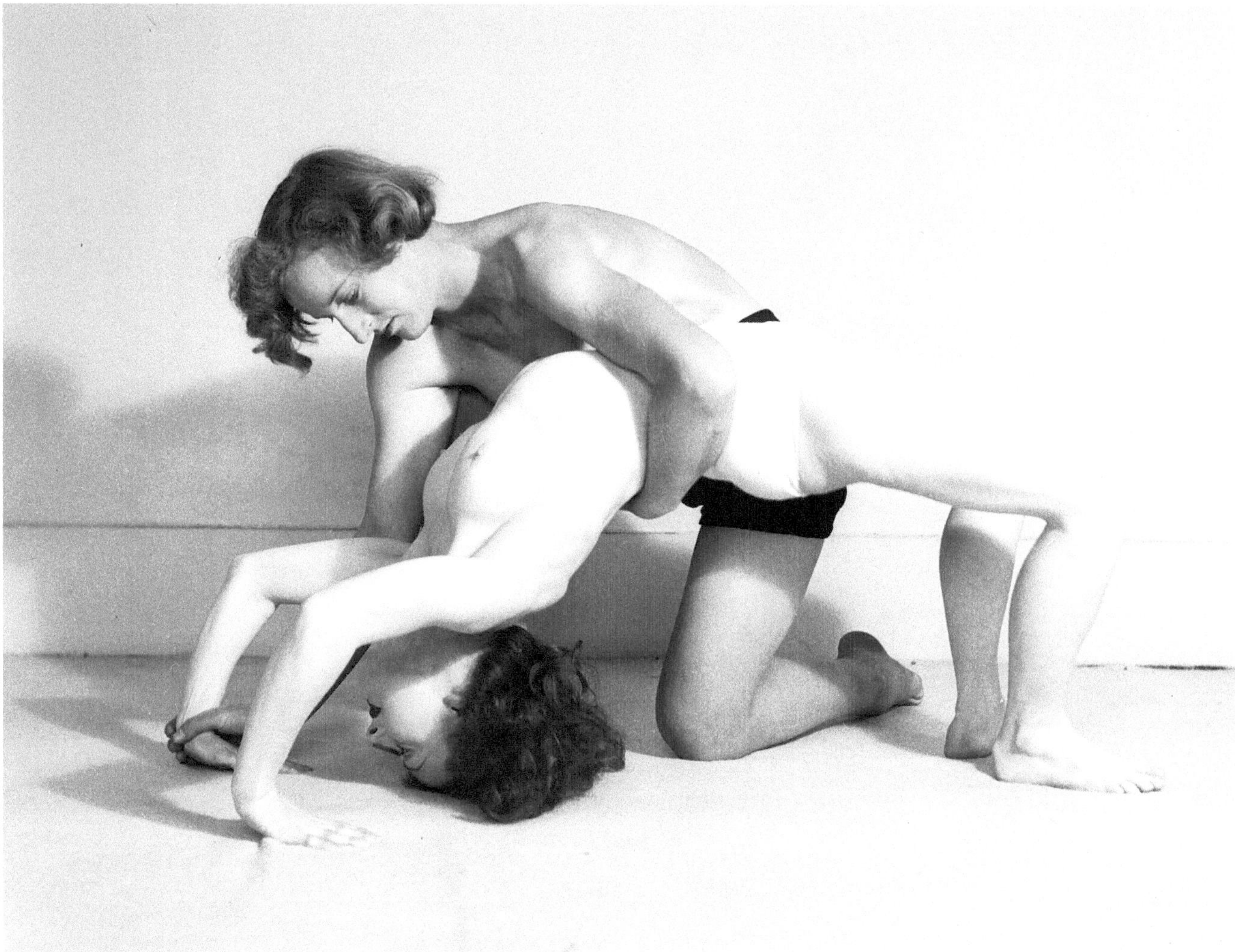

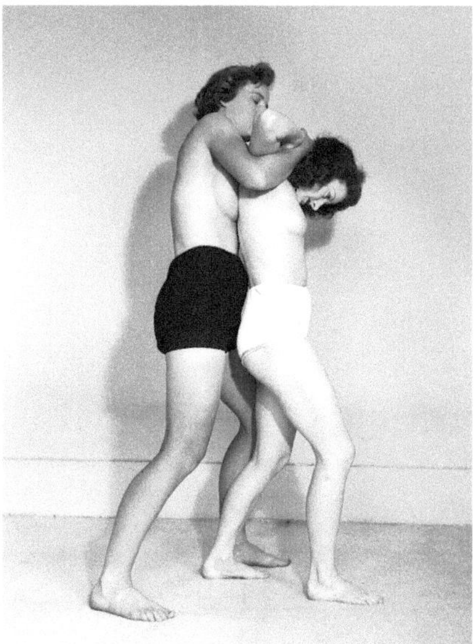

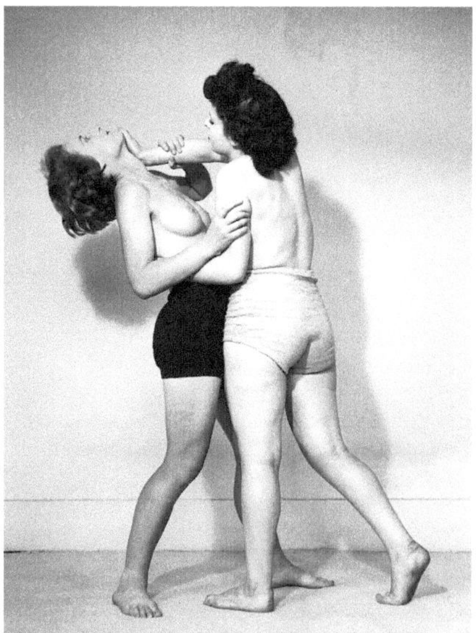

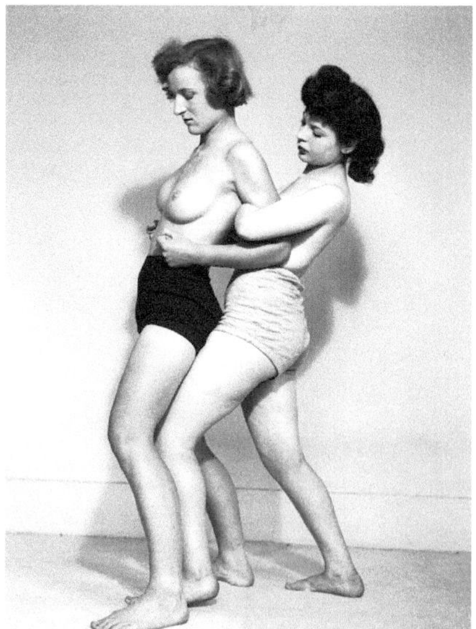

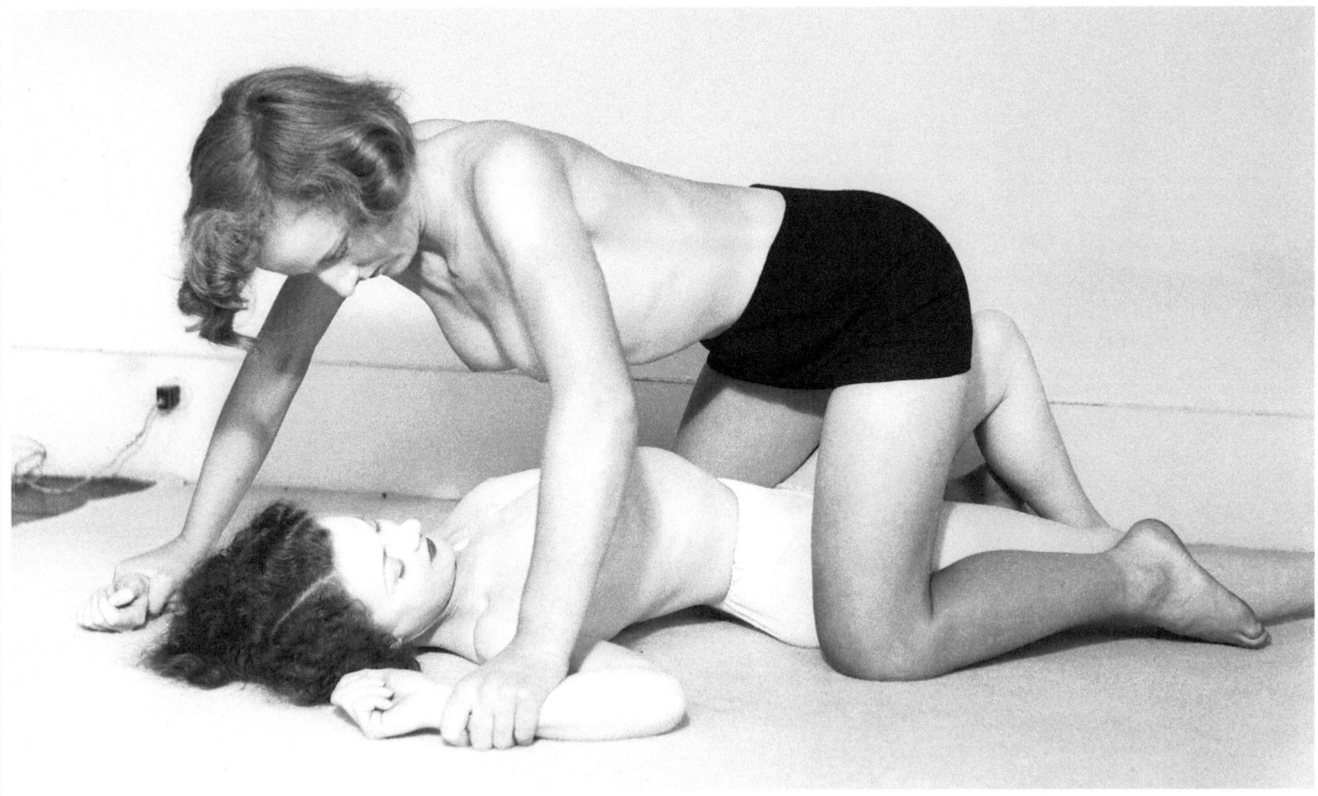

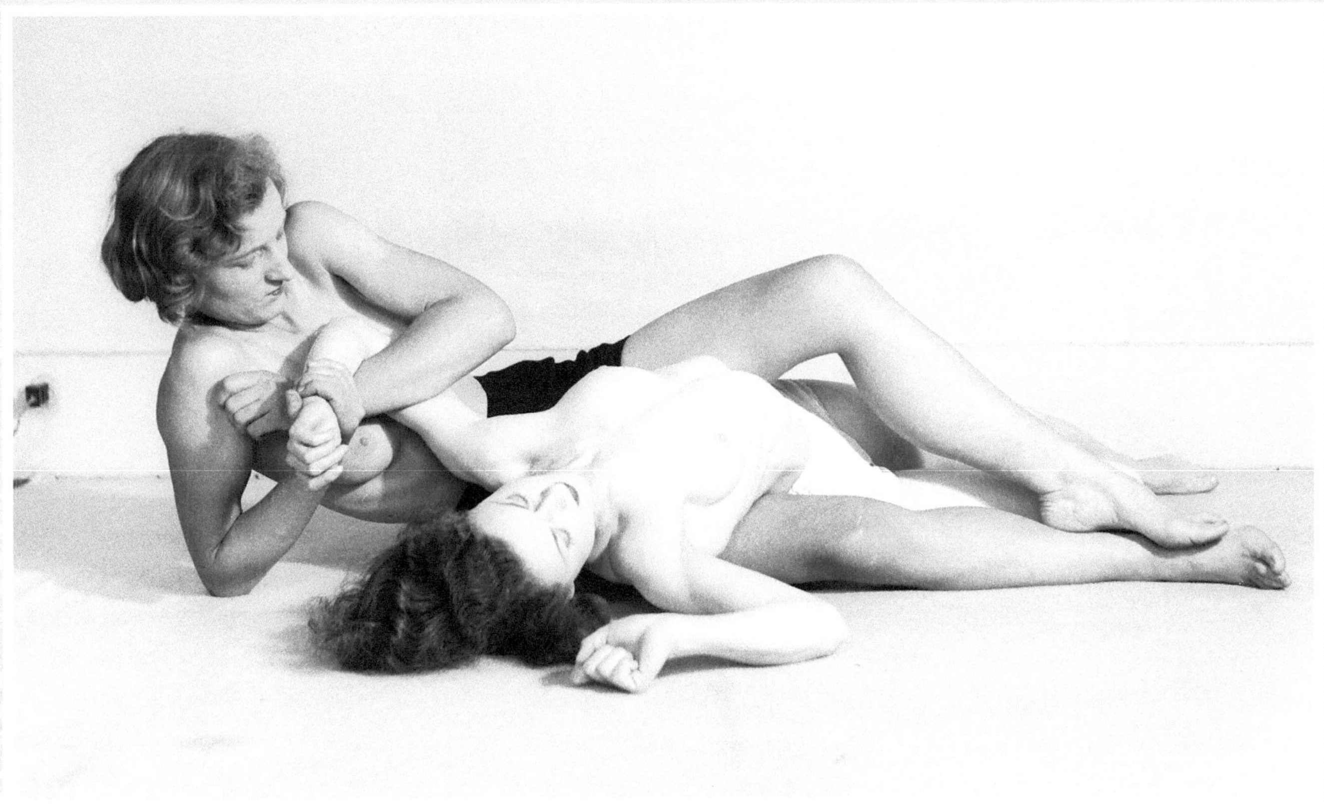

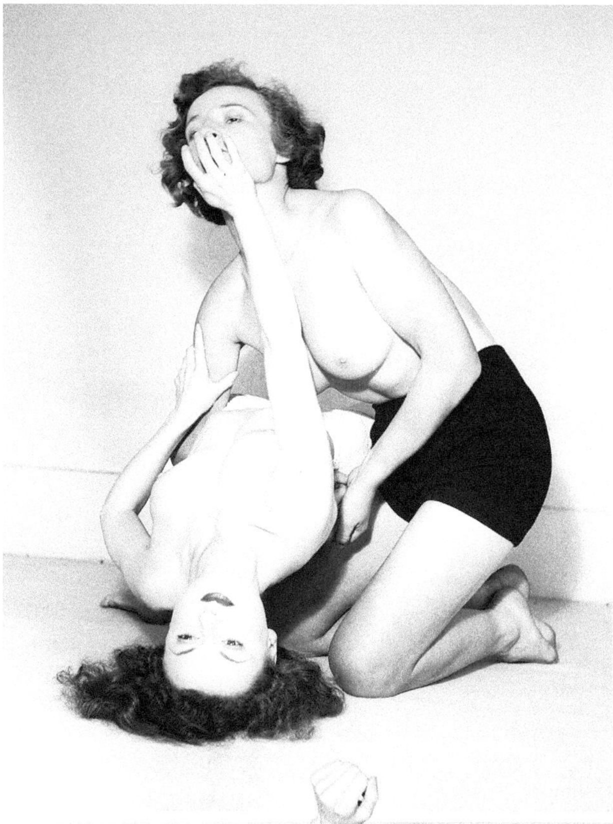
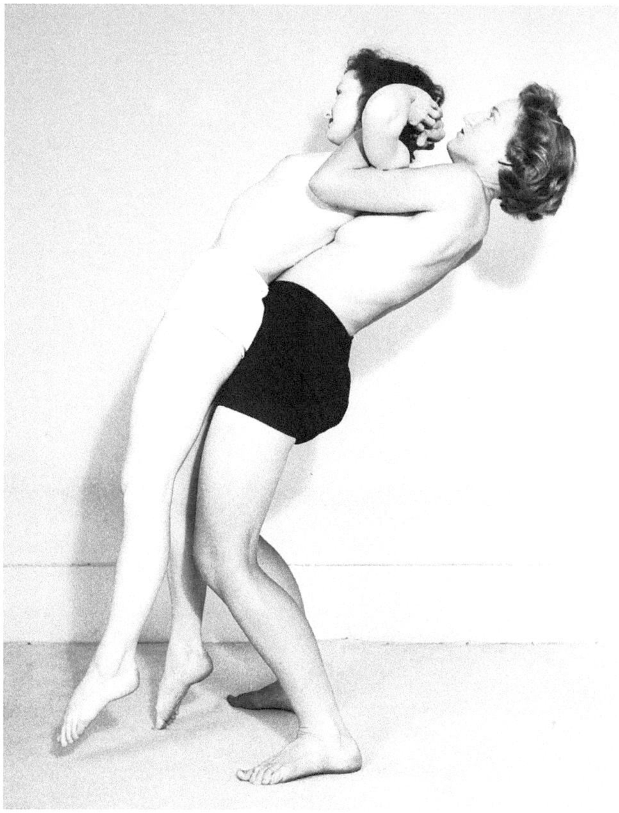
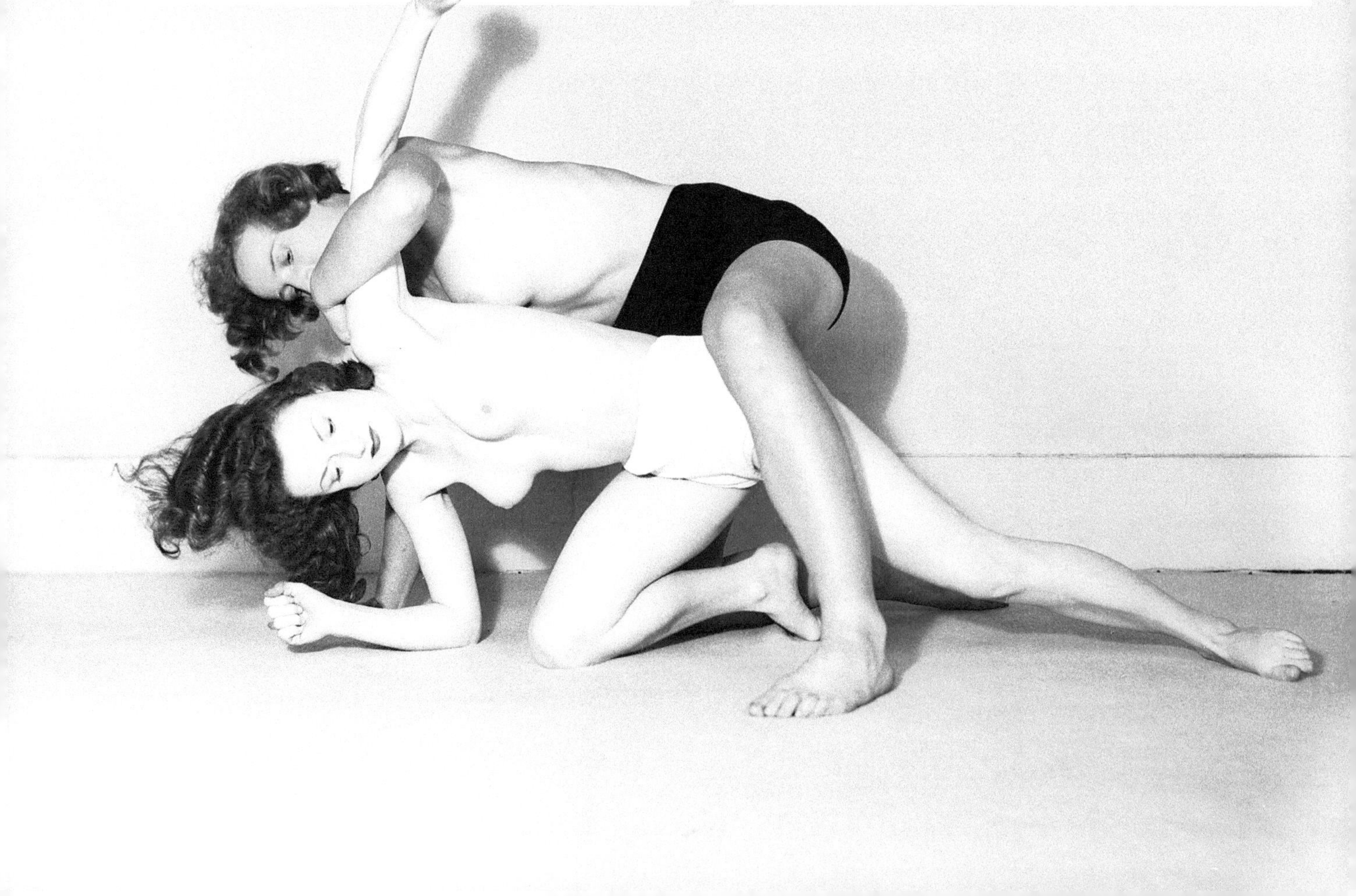

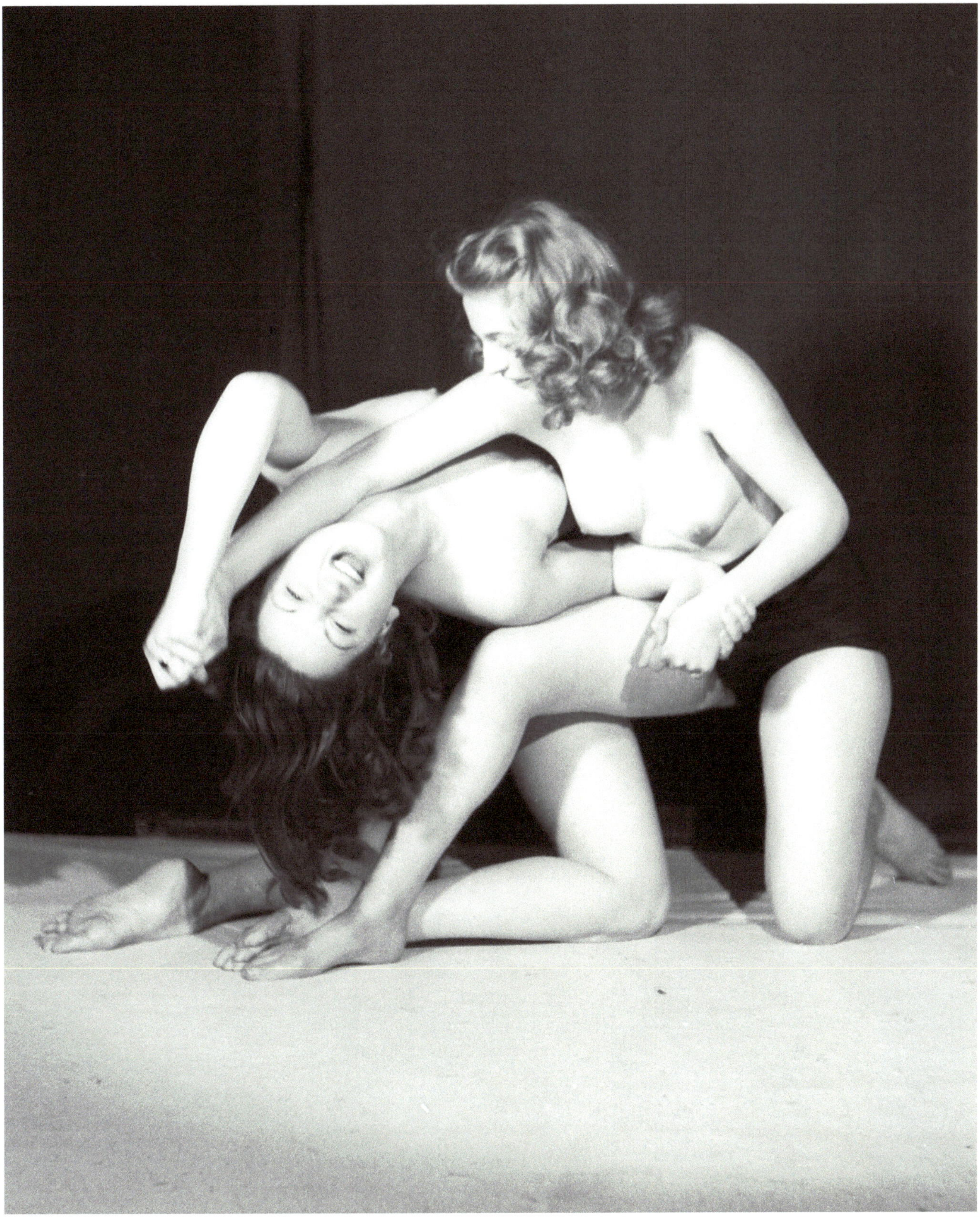

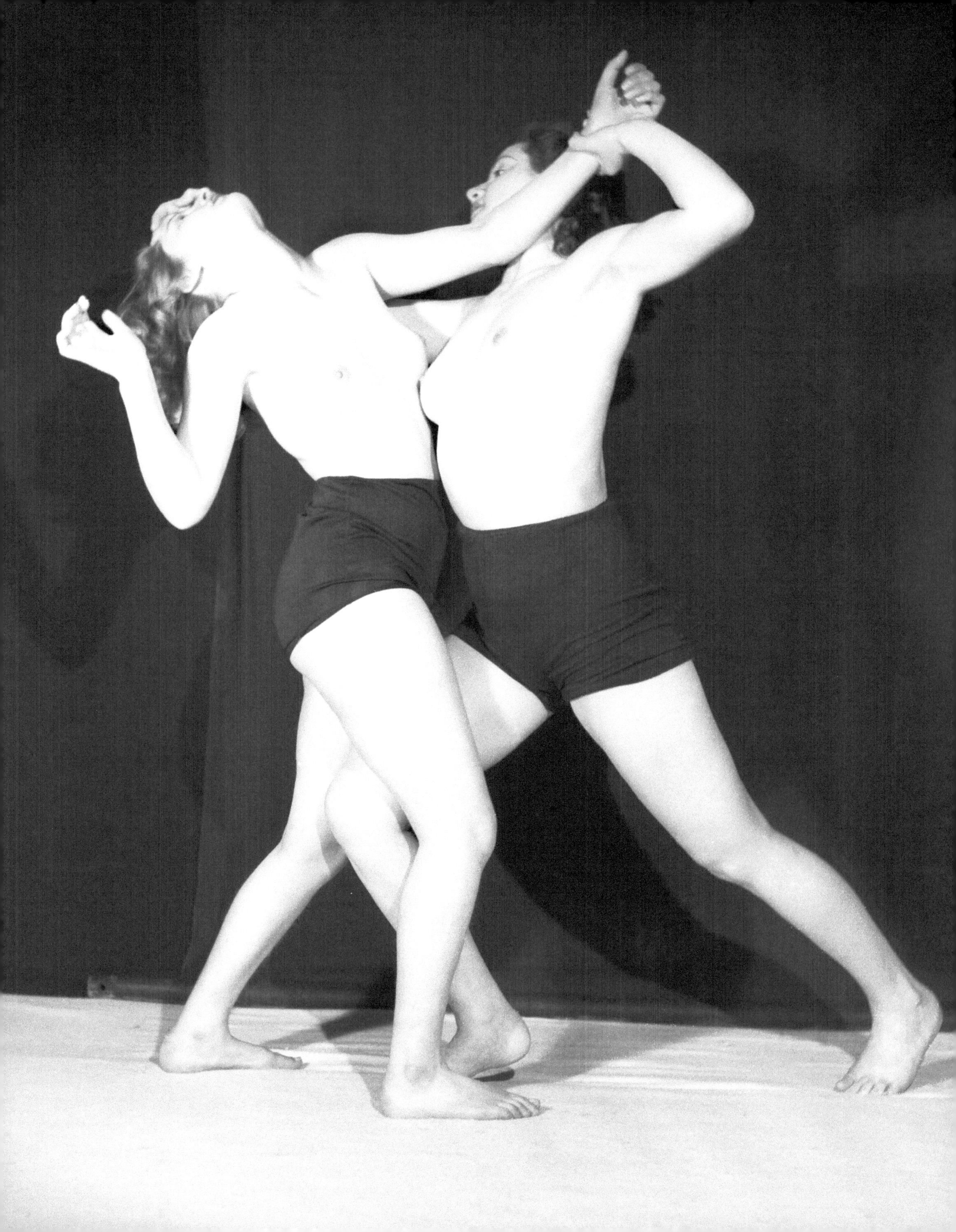

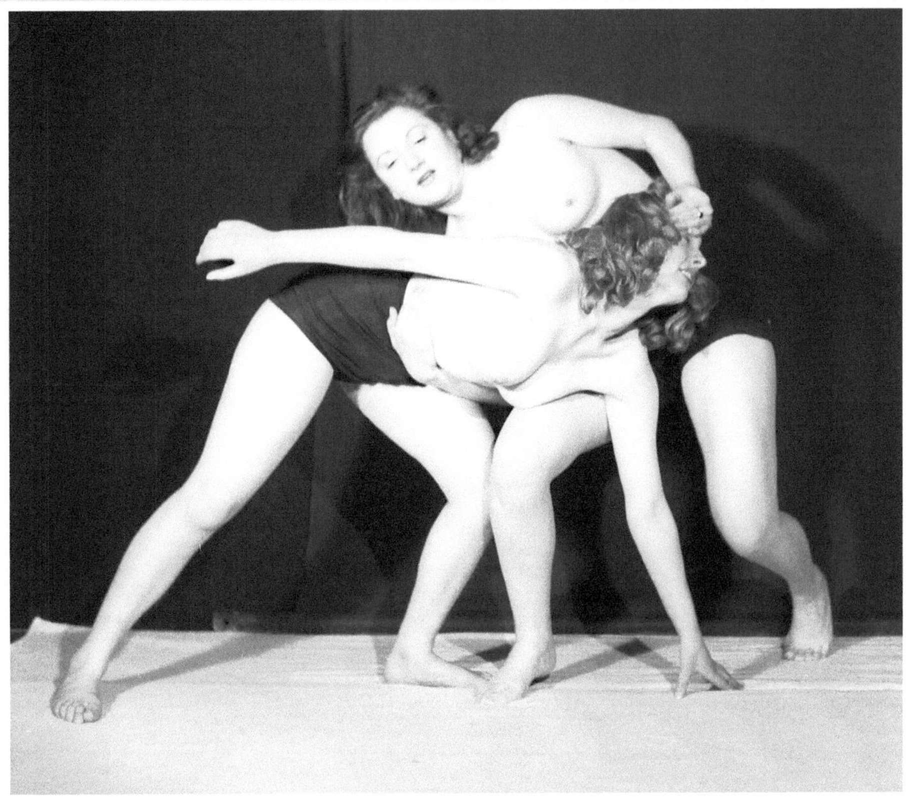

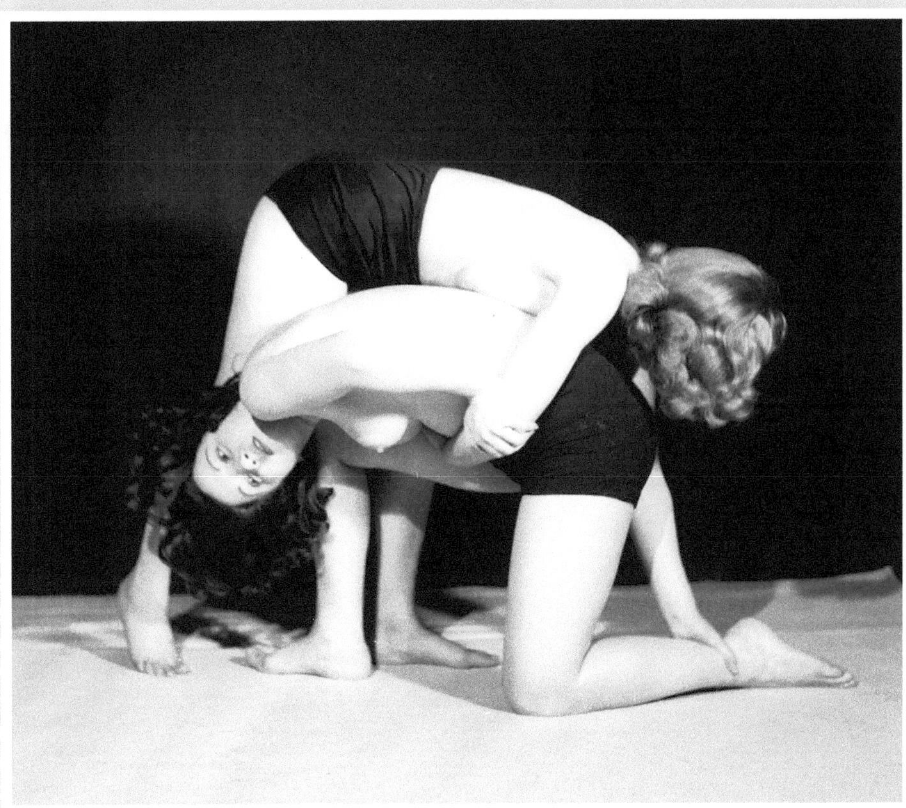

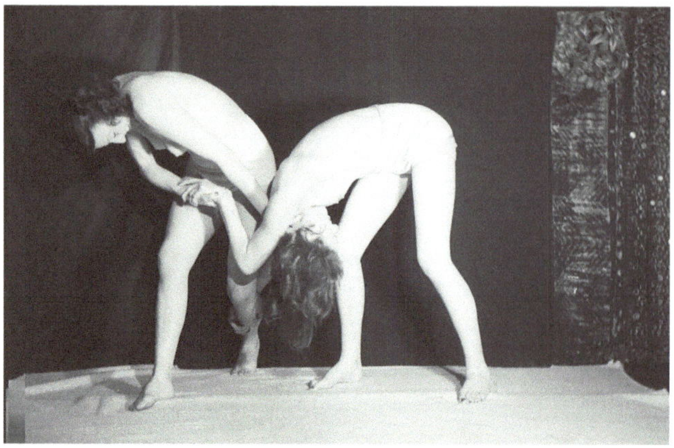
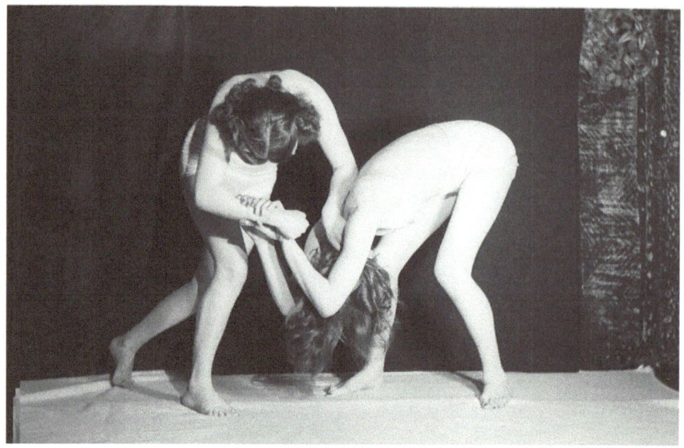
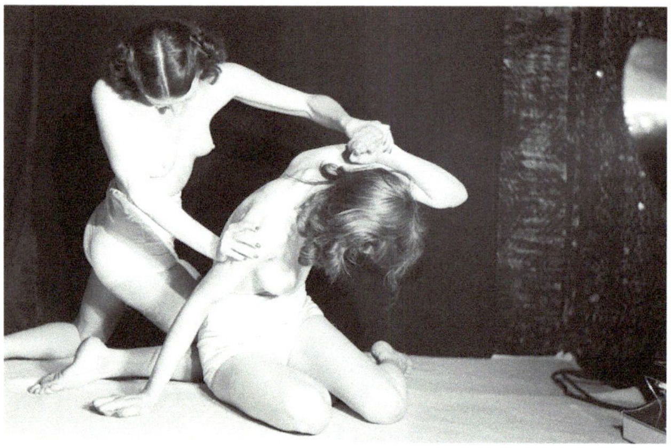
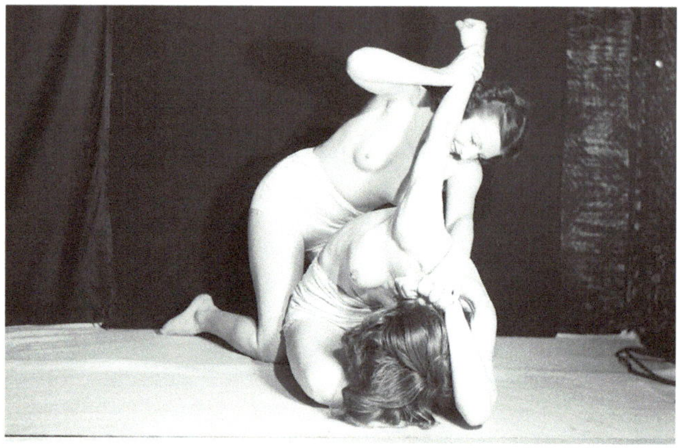
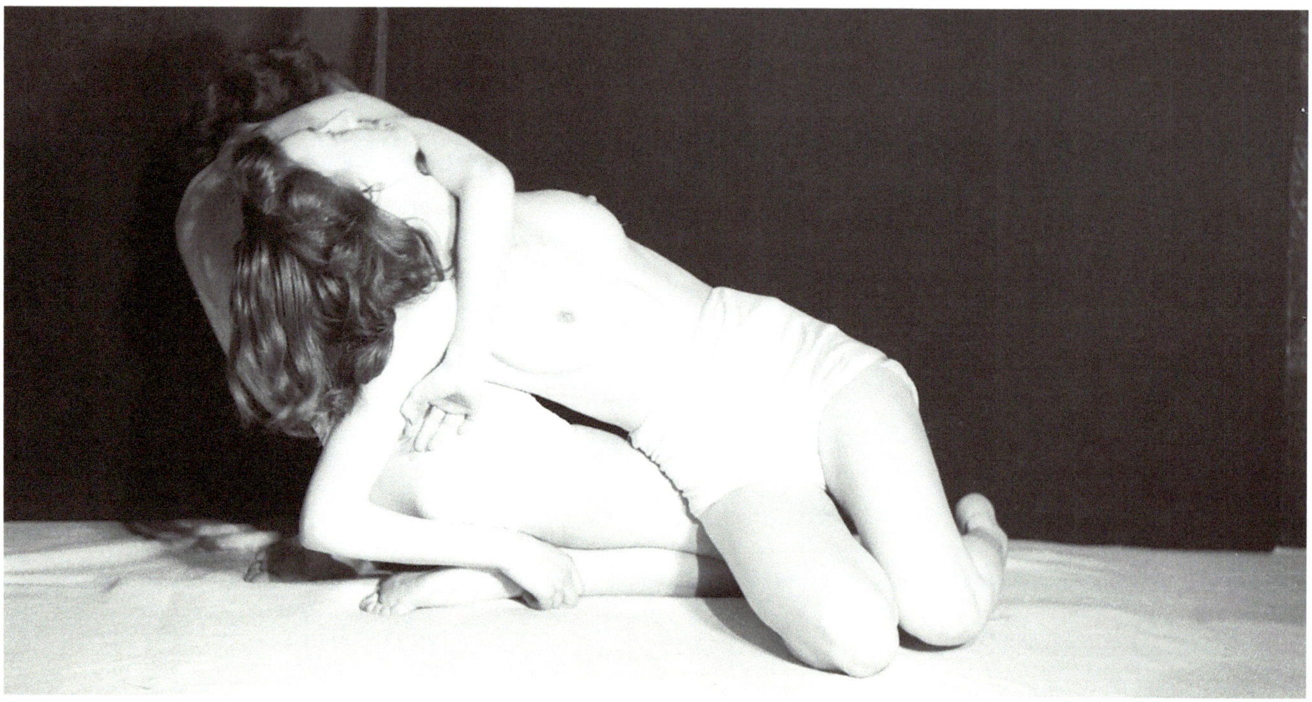

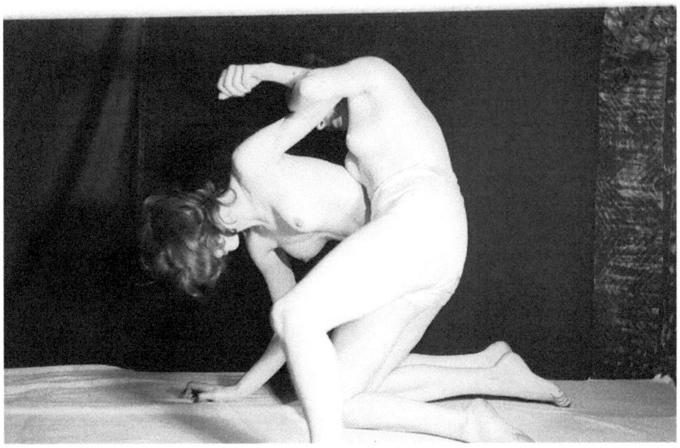
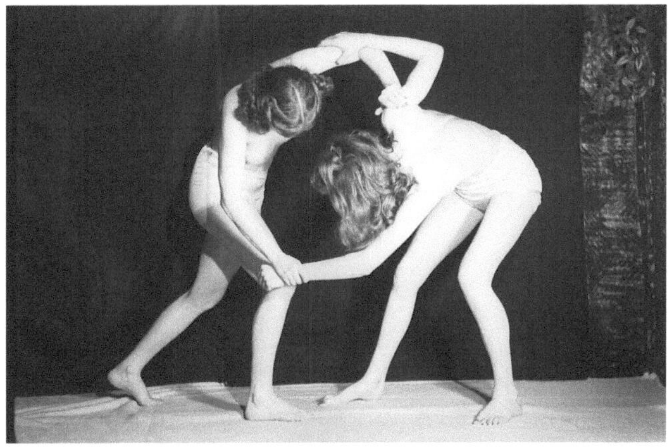
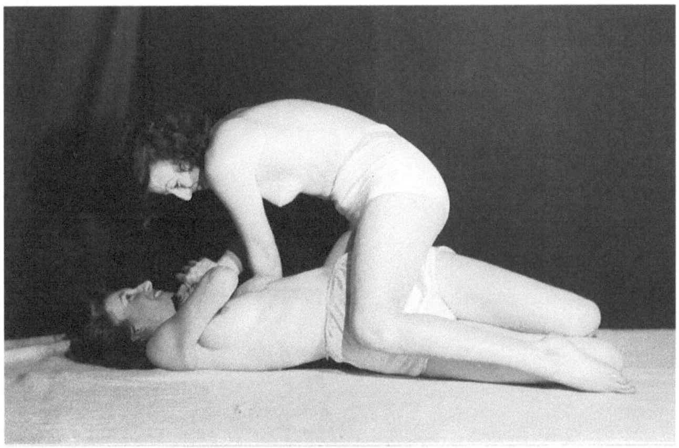
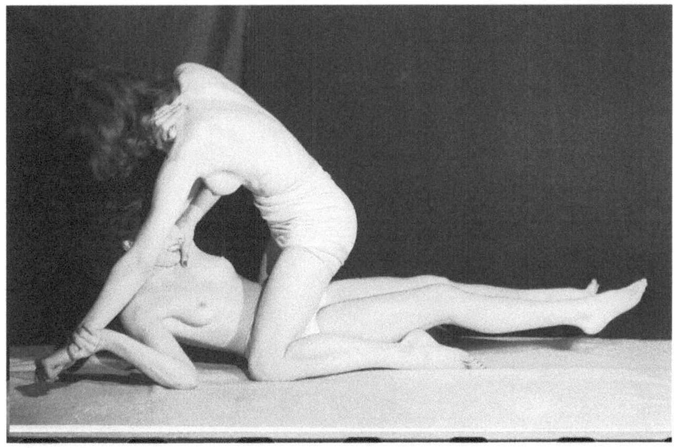
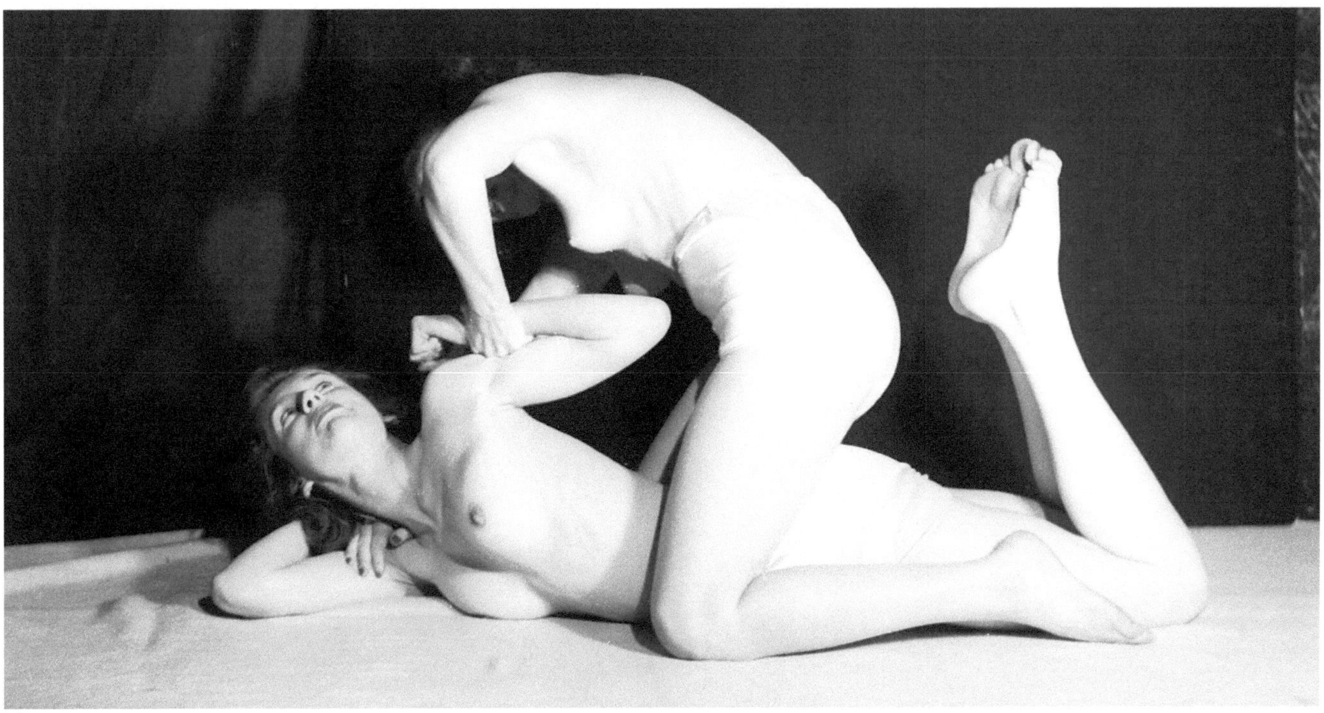

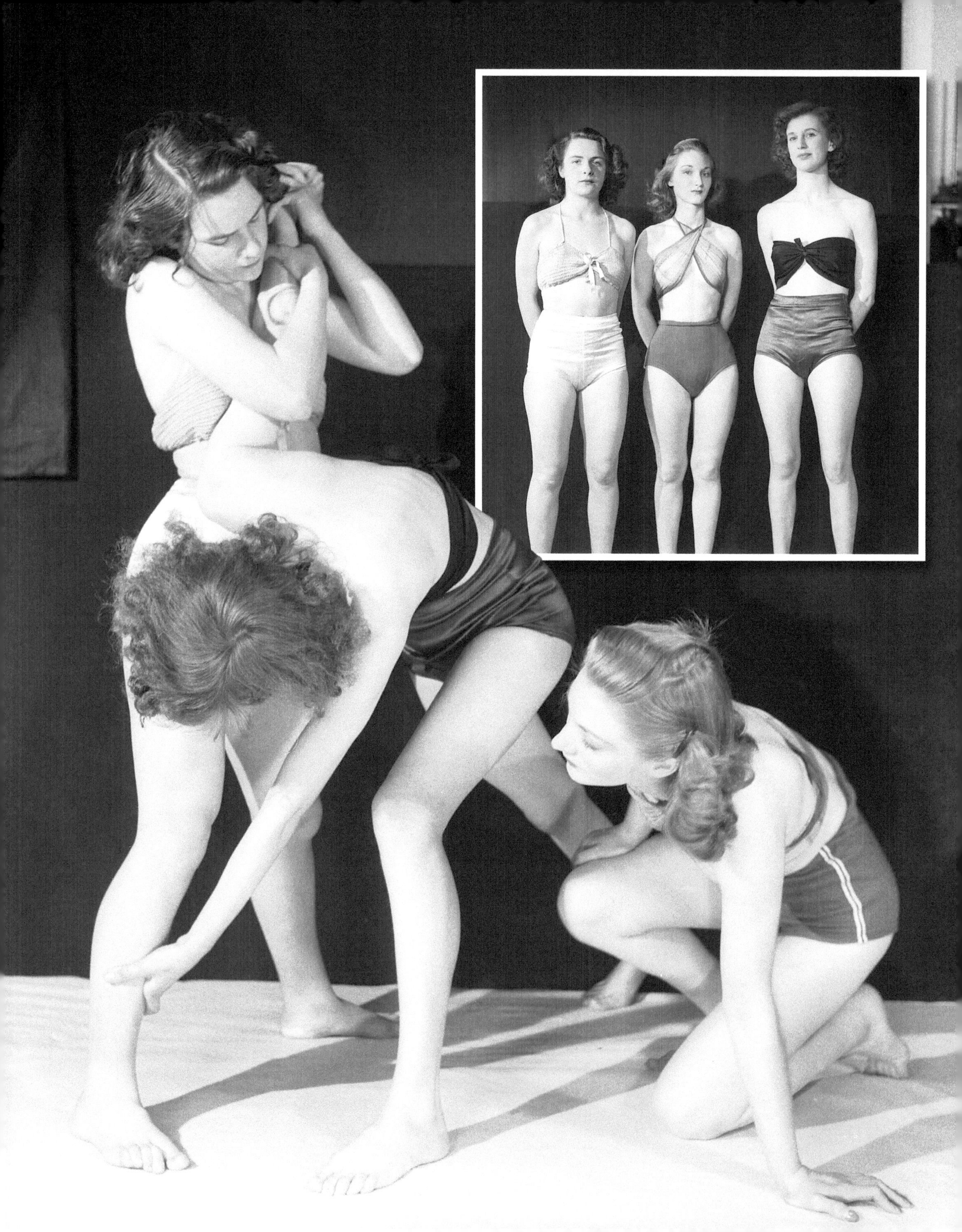

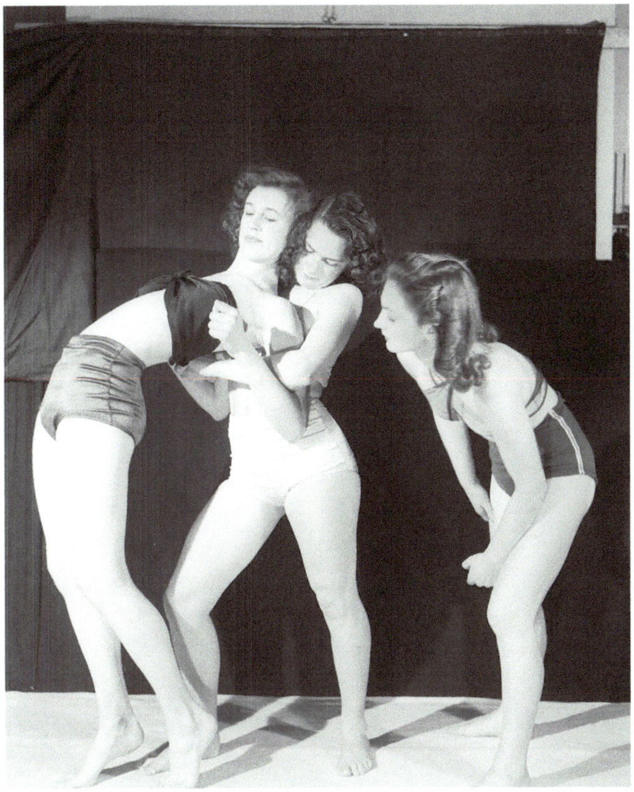

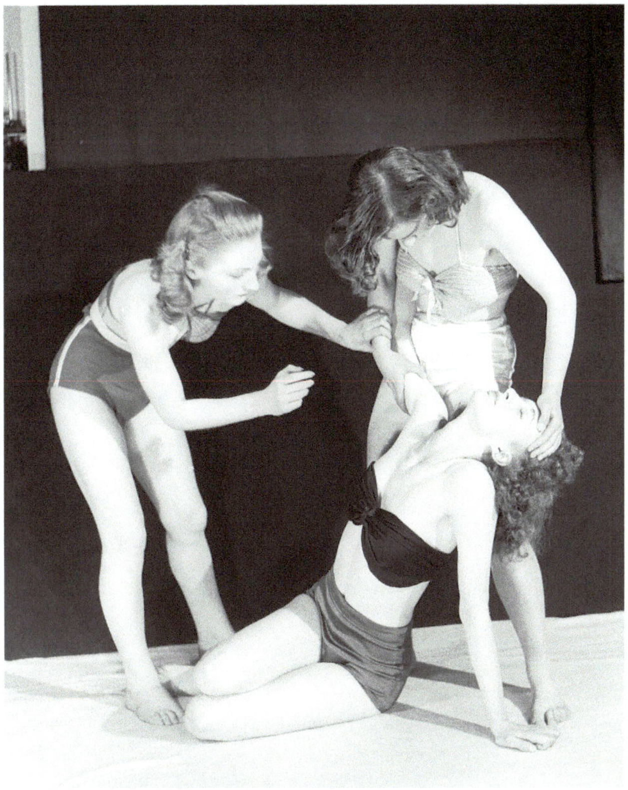

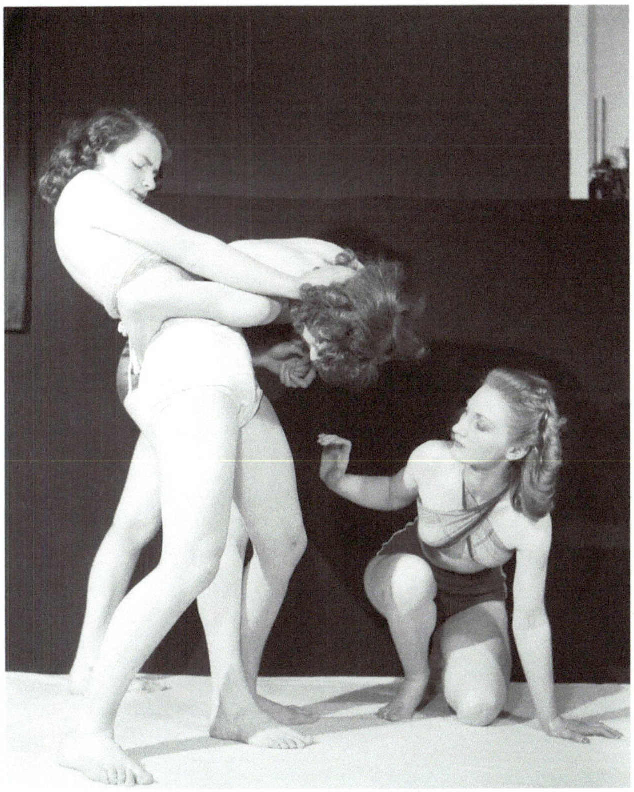

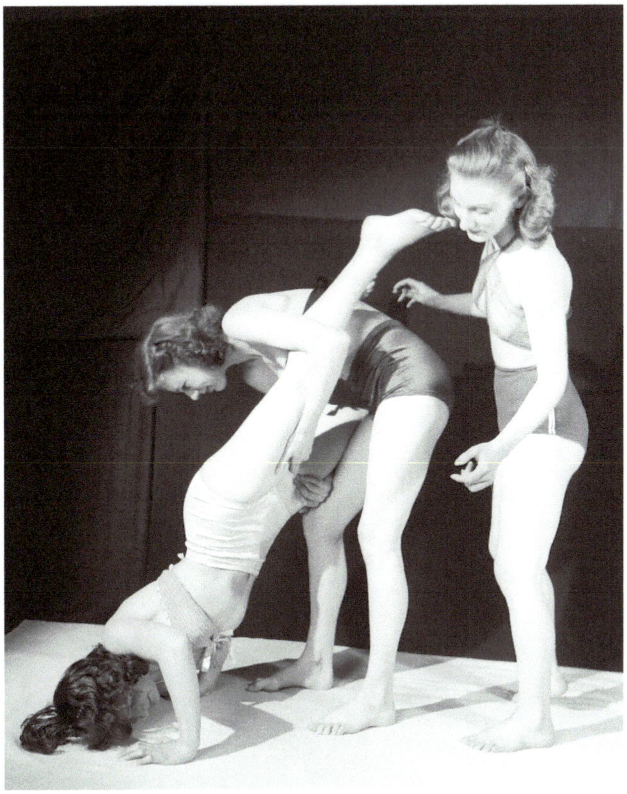

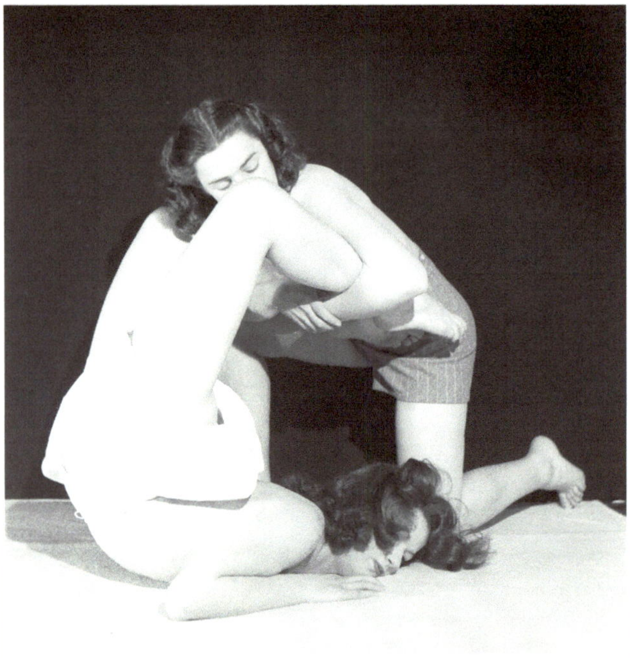

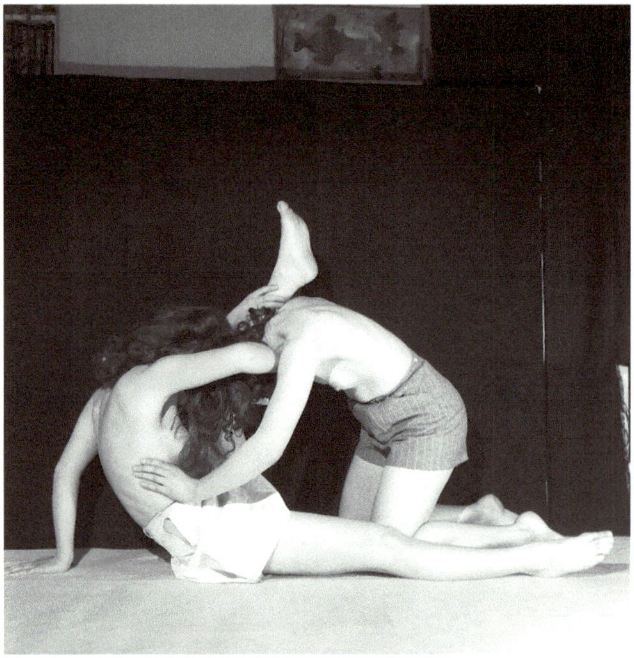

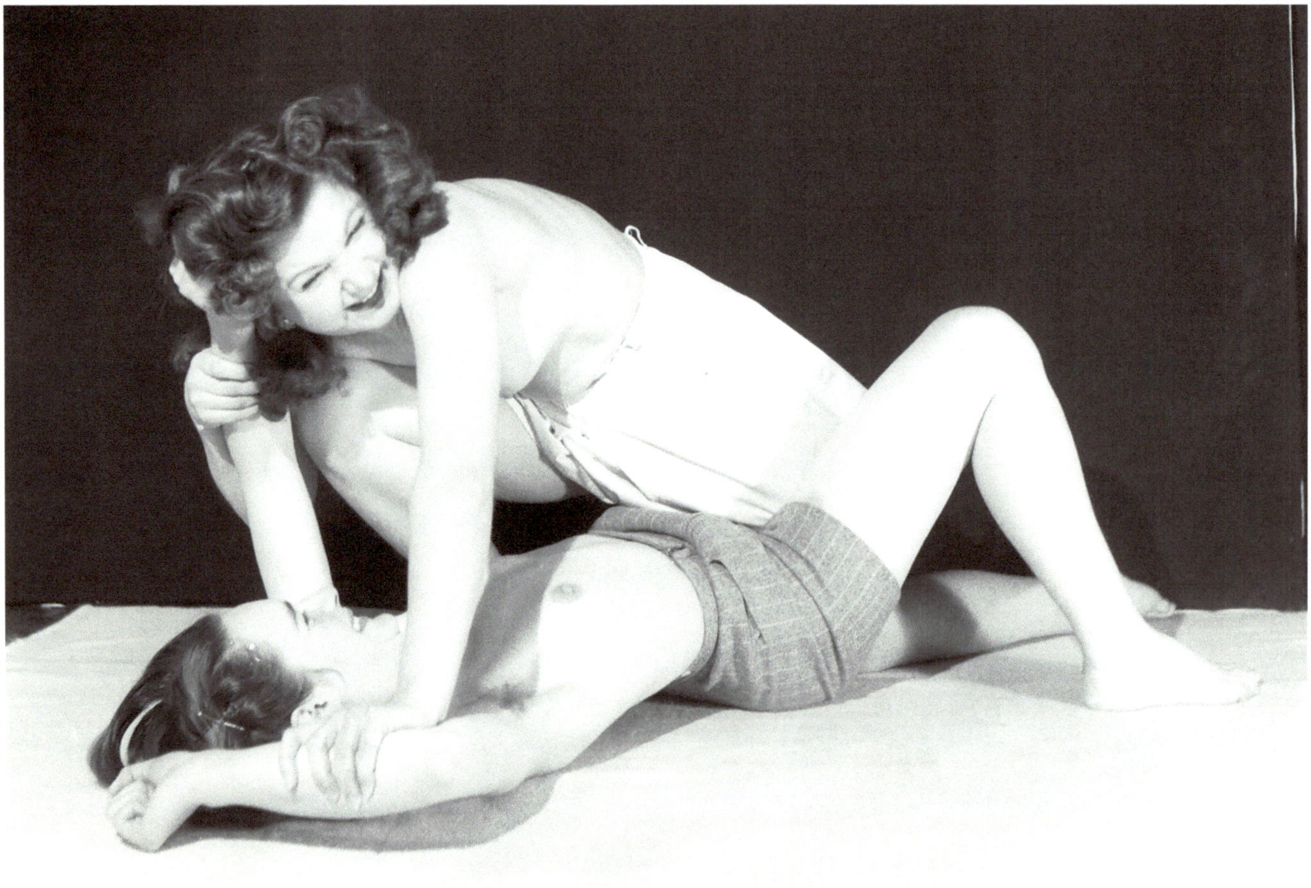

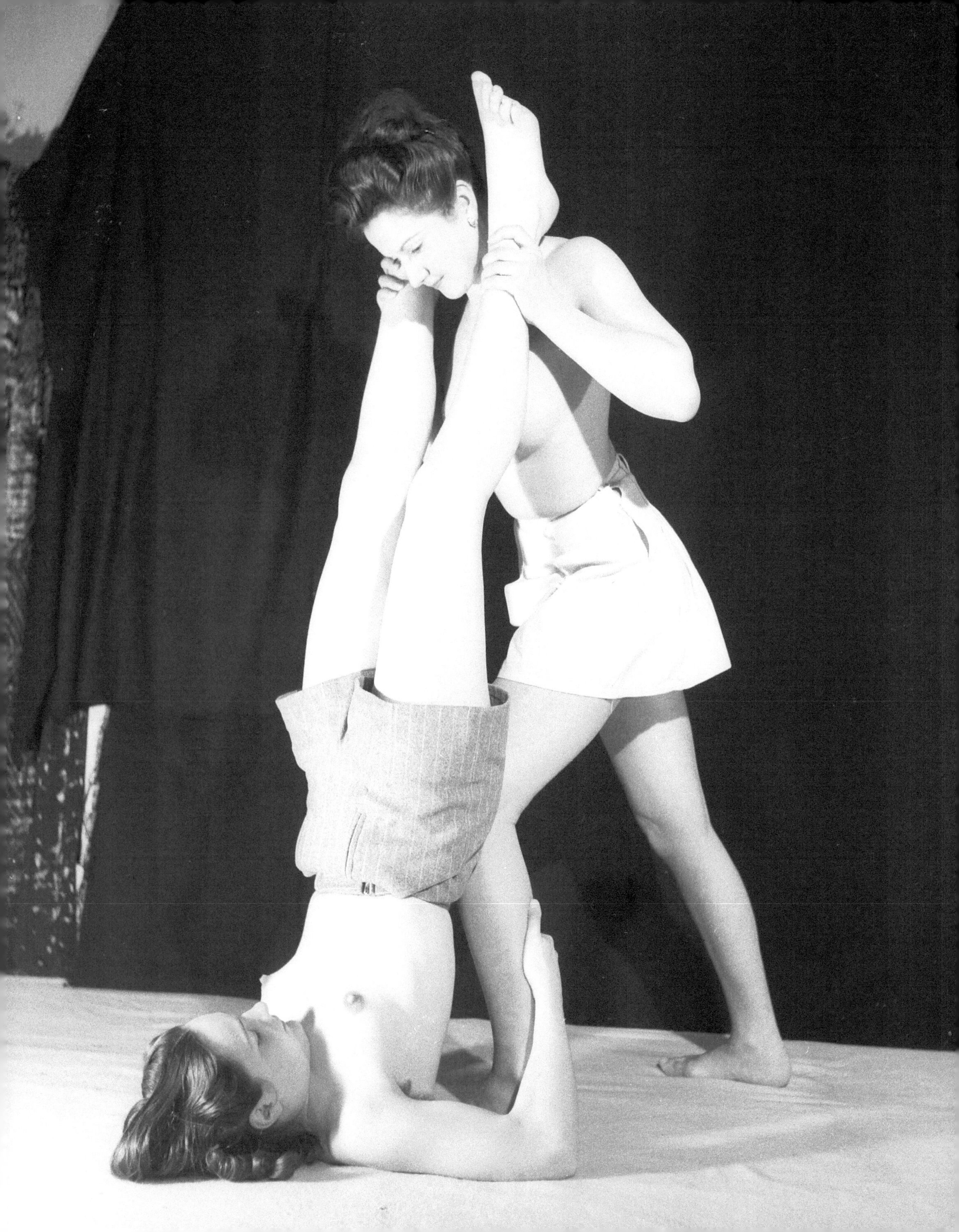

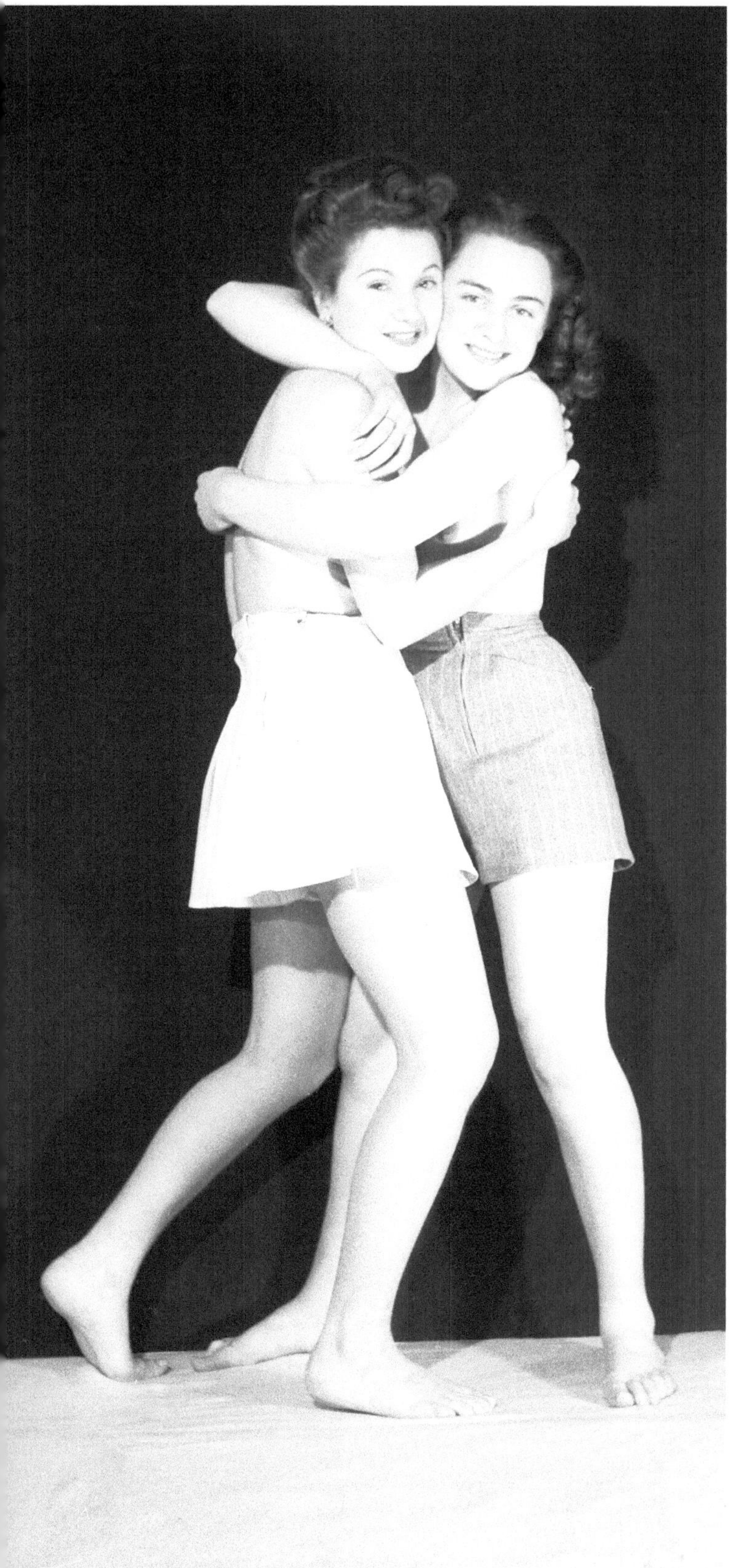

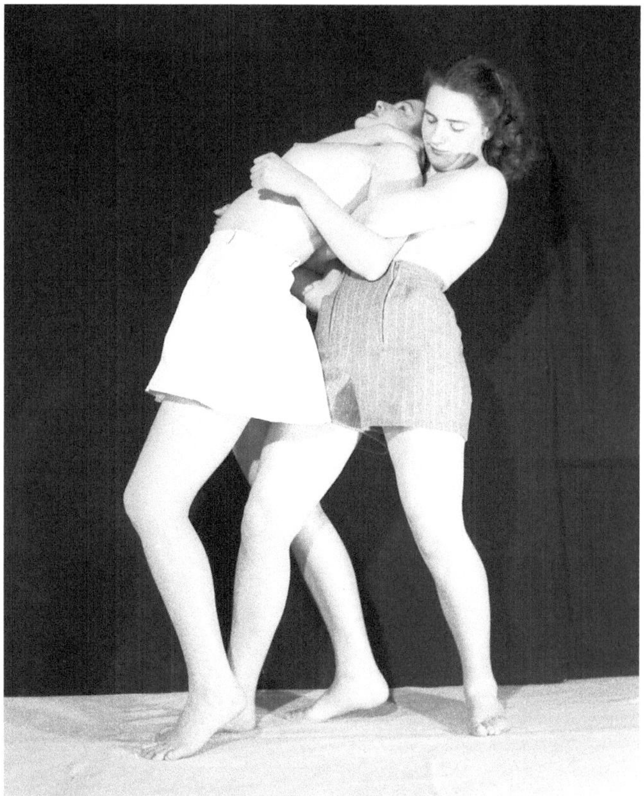

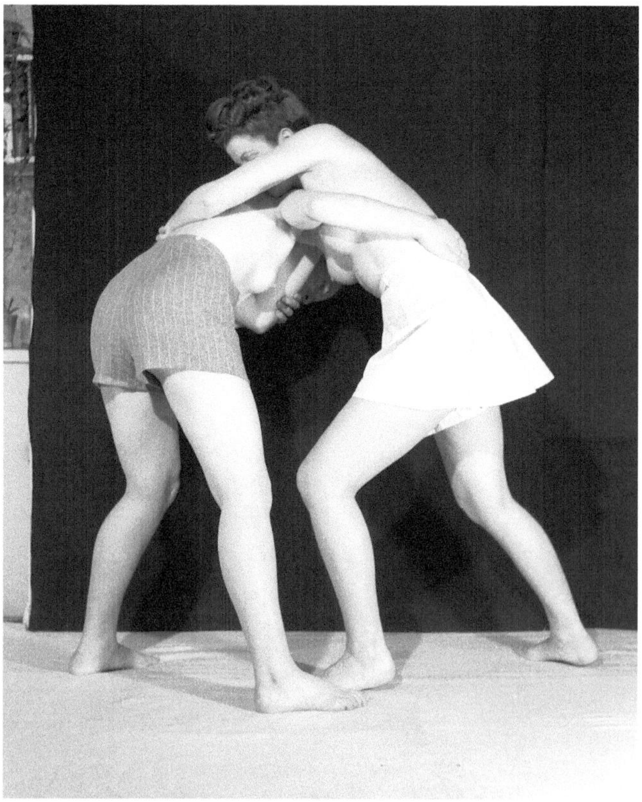

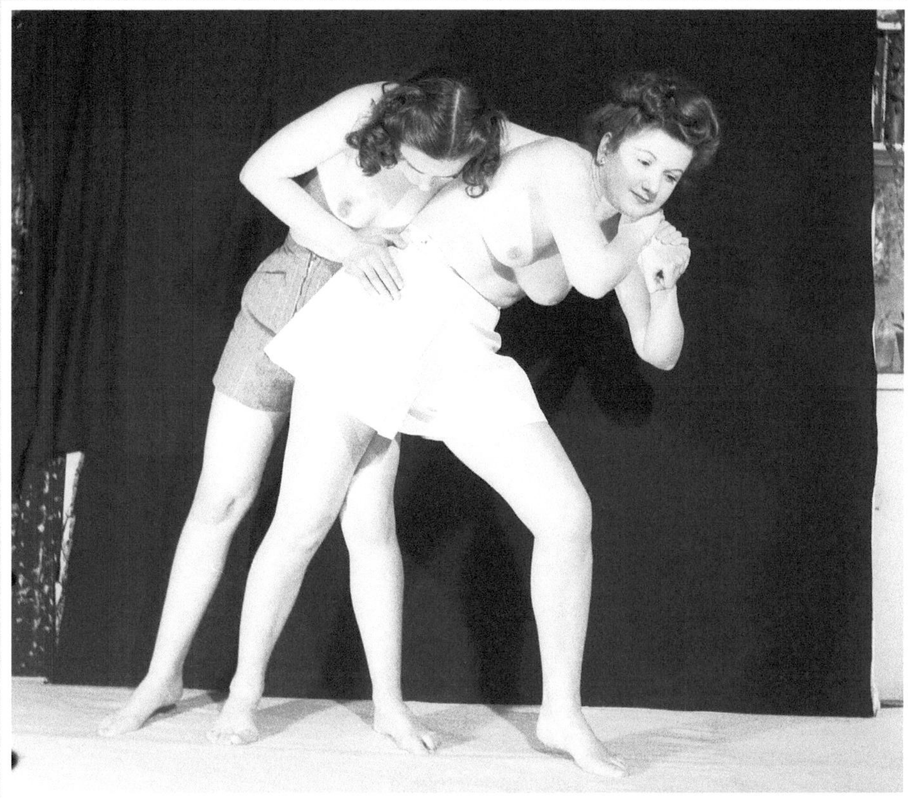

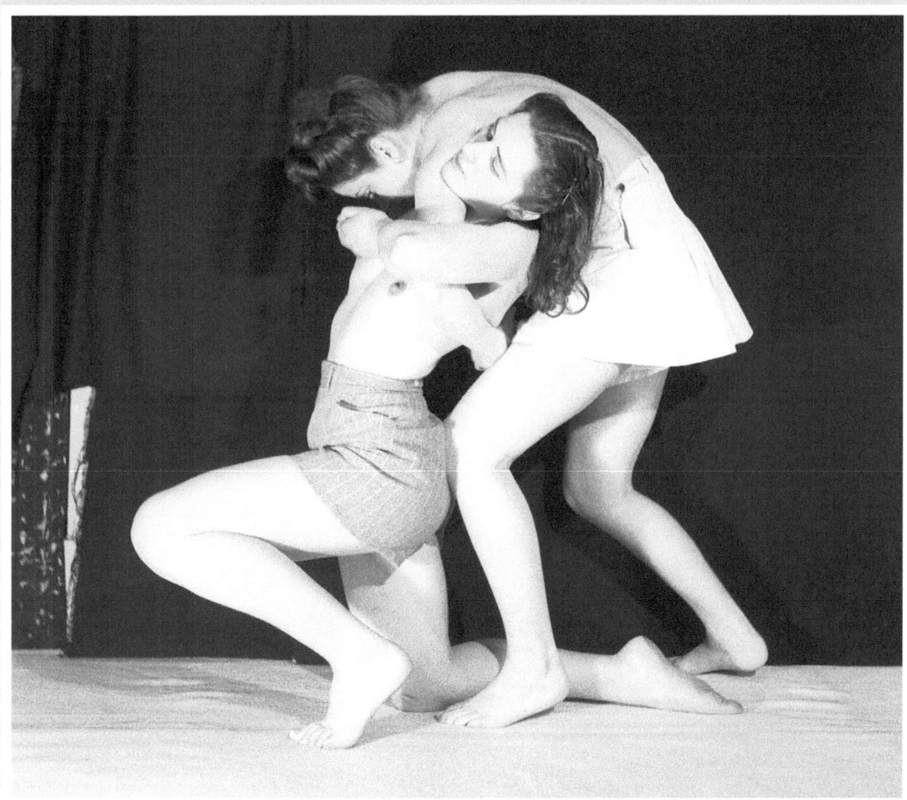

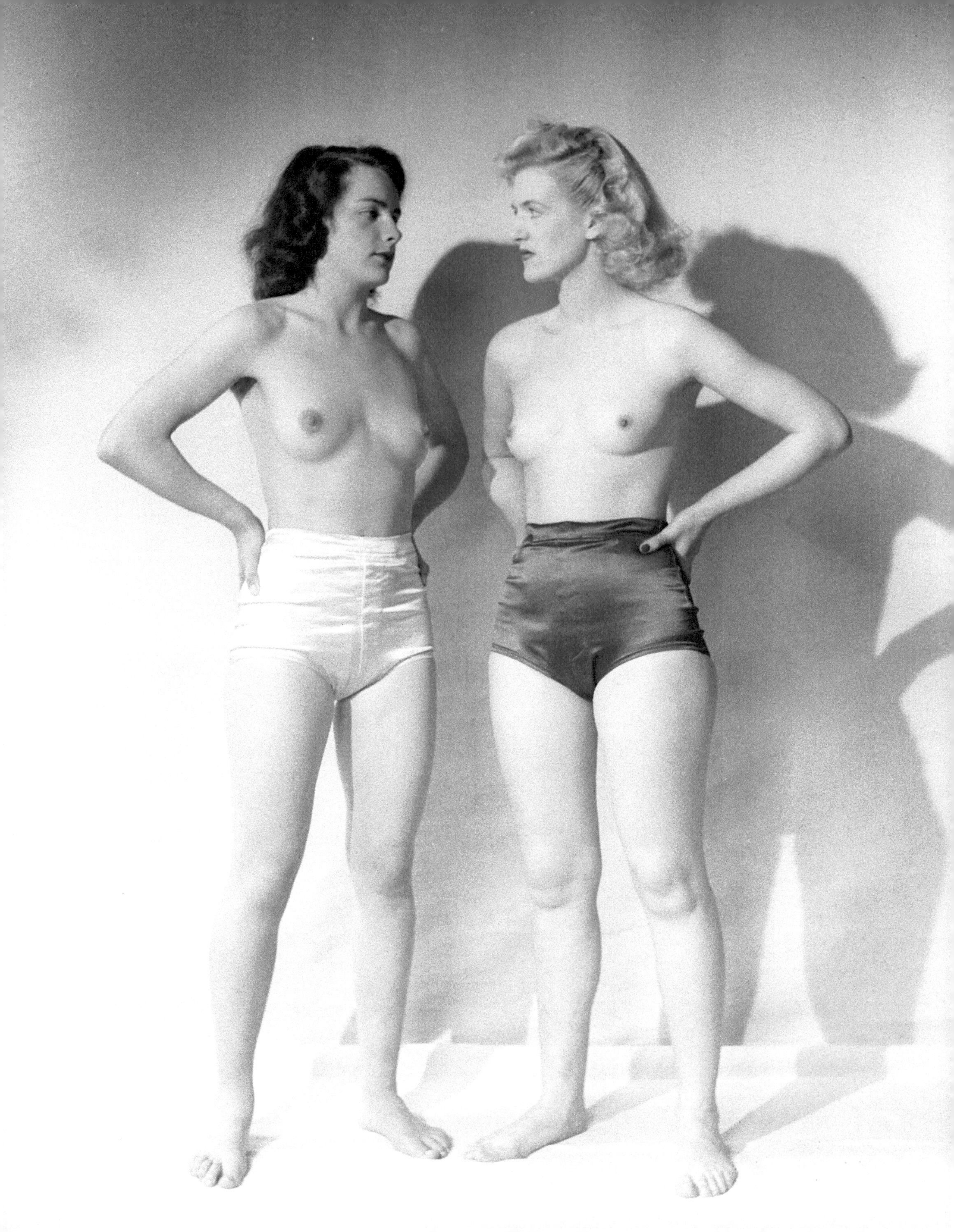

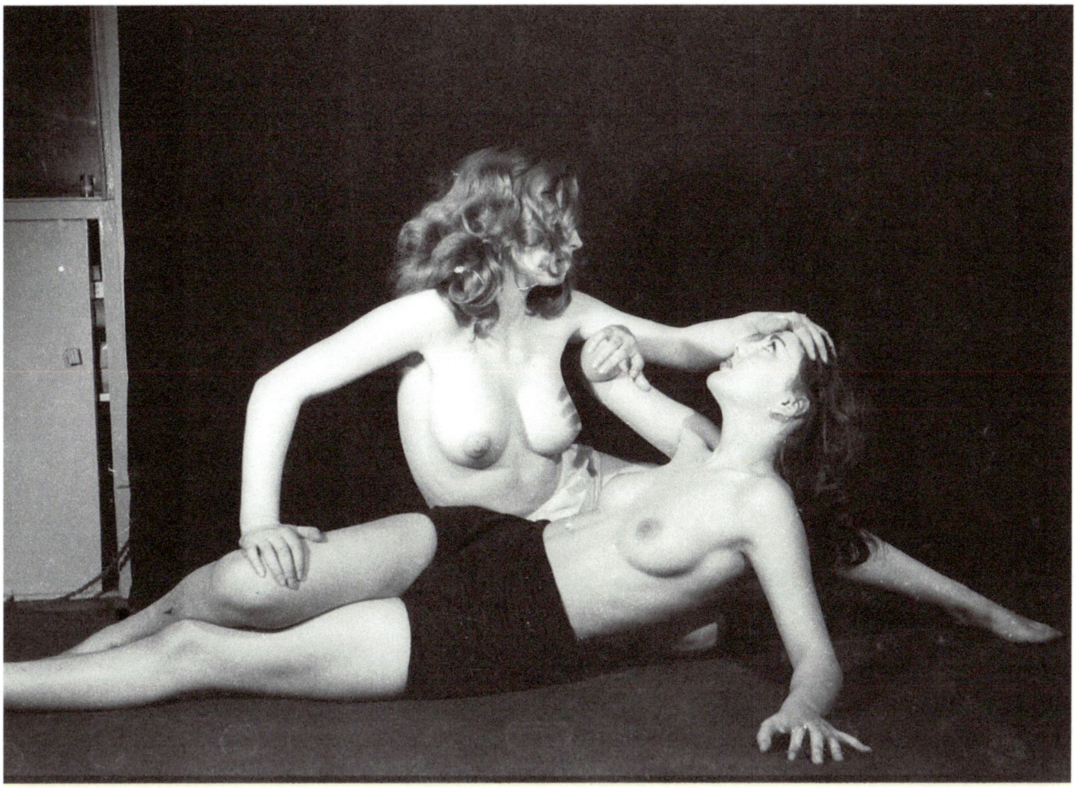

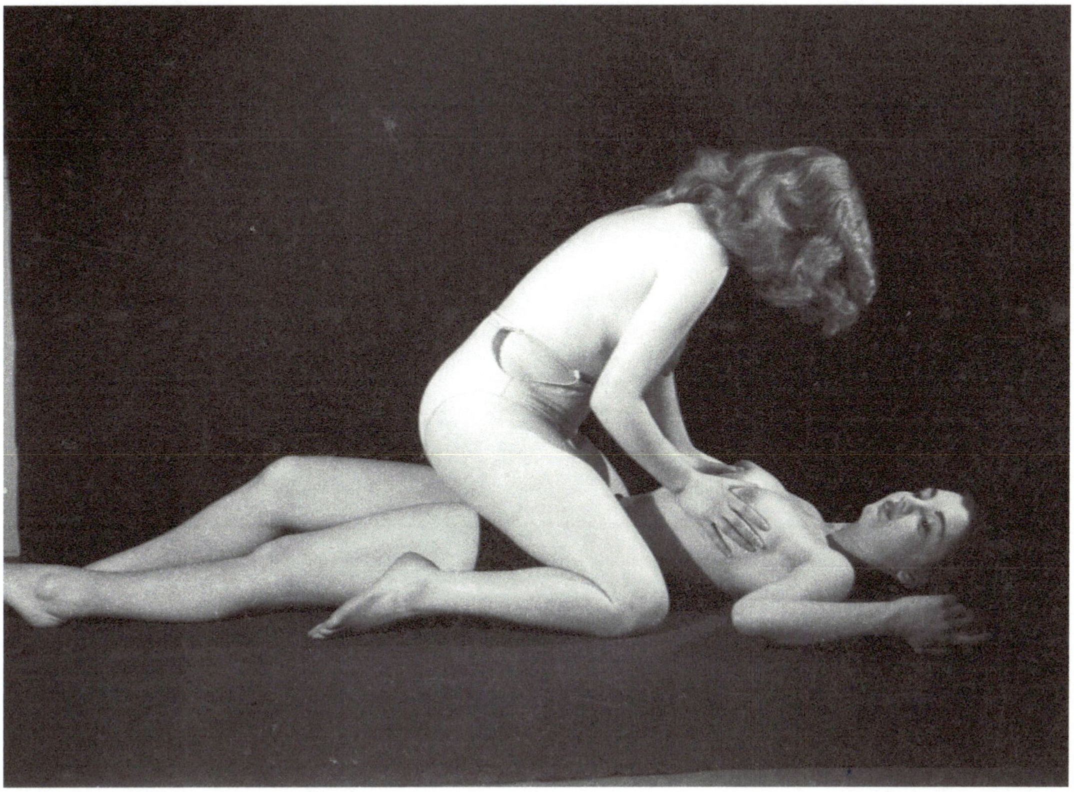

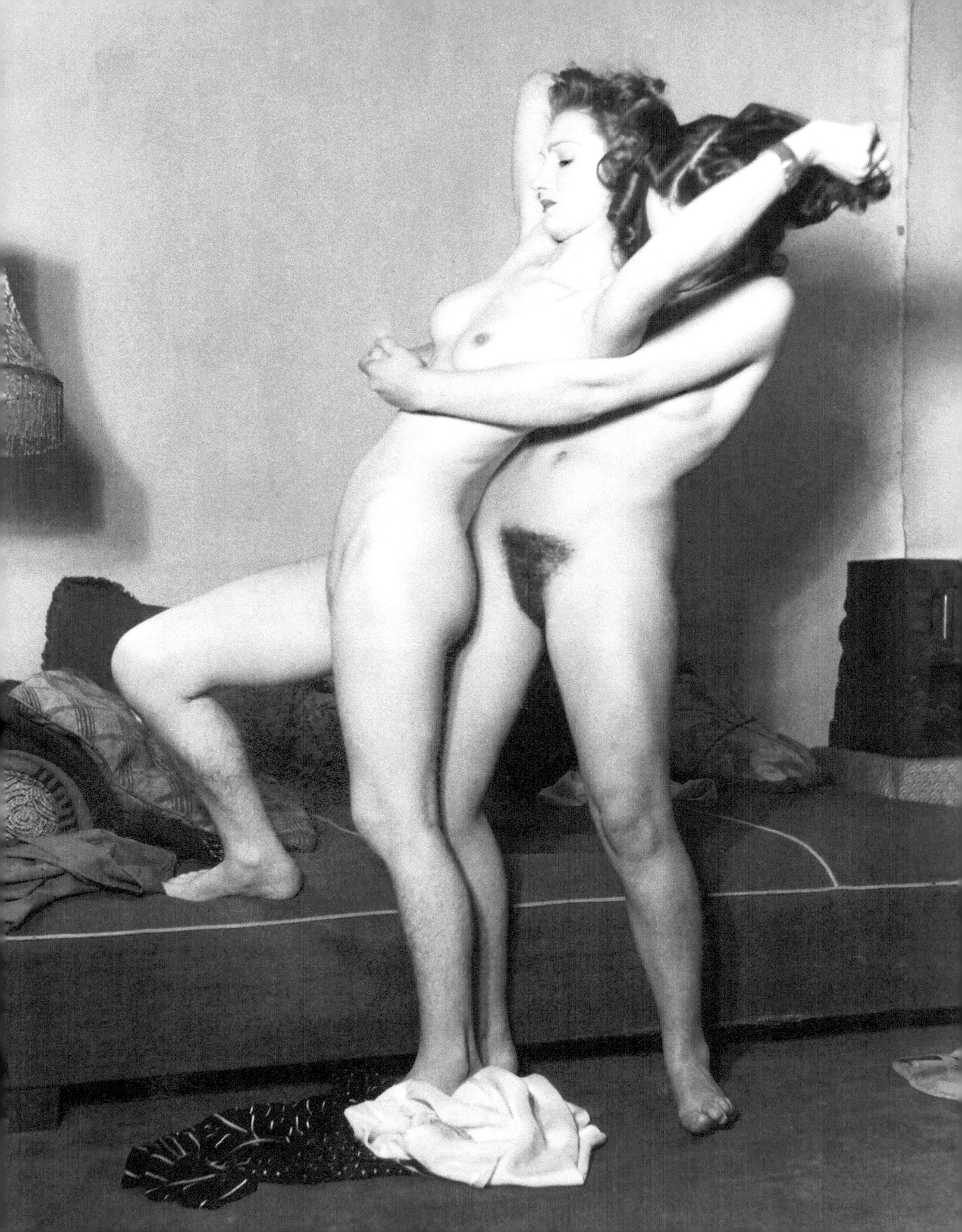

AVAILABLE TITLES FROM WOLFBAIT

Doing Rude Things
The history of the British sex film.

NEW! **Cinema au Naturel**
A history of nudist film.

Miniten: Rules of the Game
Invented in the 1930s, Miniten is a tennis-like game played by naturists.

Naked as Nature Intended
The epic tale of a nudist picture by Pamela Green, with photographs by Douglas "Dambuster" Webb, DFM.

The Naked Truth About Harrison Marks
The notorious biography by Franklyn Wood.

Past Masters of the Nude
An illustrated bibliography of nude photography books published in England from 1896 to 1960.

THE STEPHEN GLASS COLLECTION

Amazons of Yesteryear
A rare, action-packed collection of images of wrestling women of the 1940s and 1950s.

Beauty Off-Duty
Relaxed, everyday moments caught on camera.

Naked in the Menagerie
A playful look at Eve accompanied by her animal friends.

Nudist Camp Follies – volumes 1 and 2
An intimate look at the natural and free atmosphere in Sun Clubs.

Nymphs and Naiads
Beauty unadorned and outdoors.

NEW! **Poise and Pose**
A magnificent series of photographs of female beauty taken in the studio.

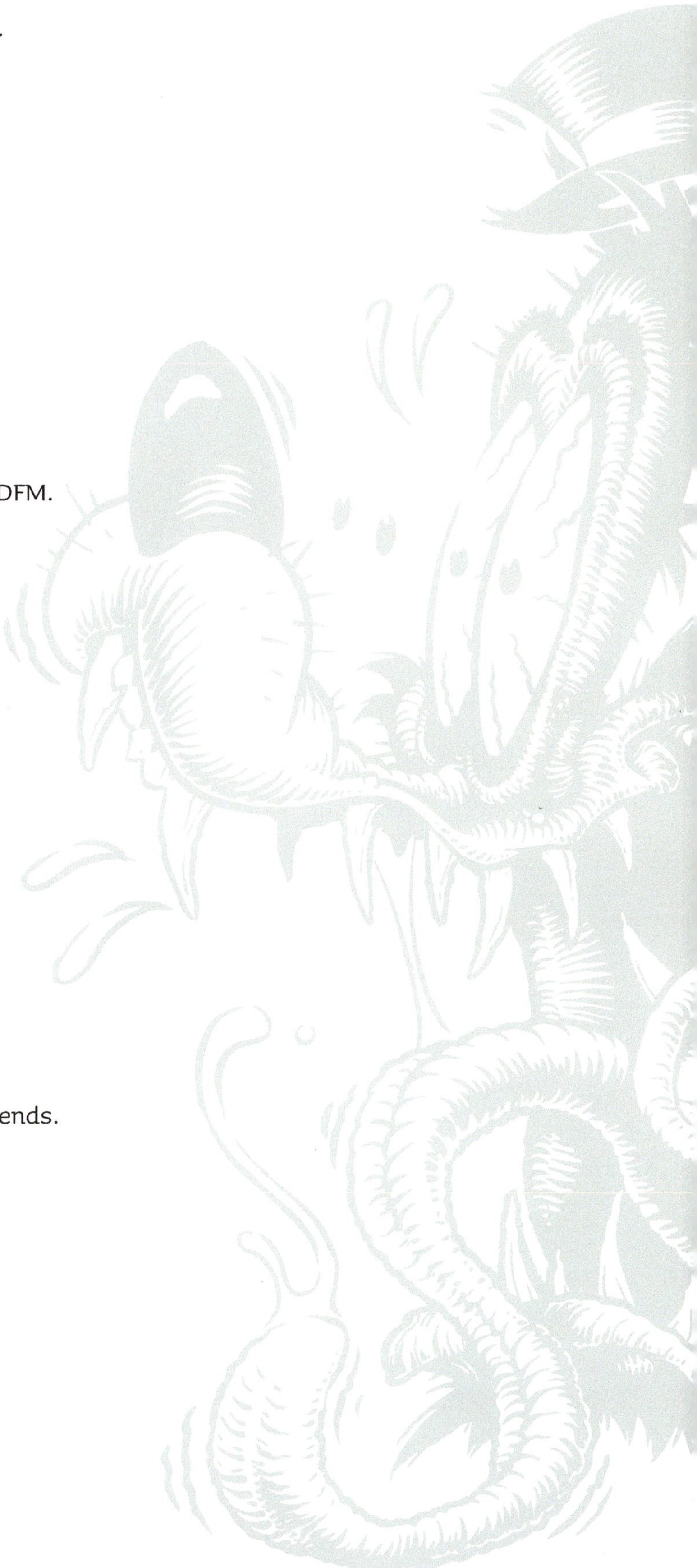

Order online at wolfbait.co.uk

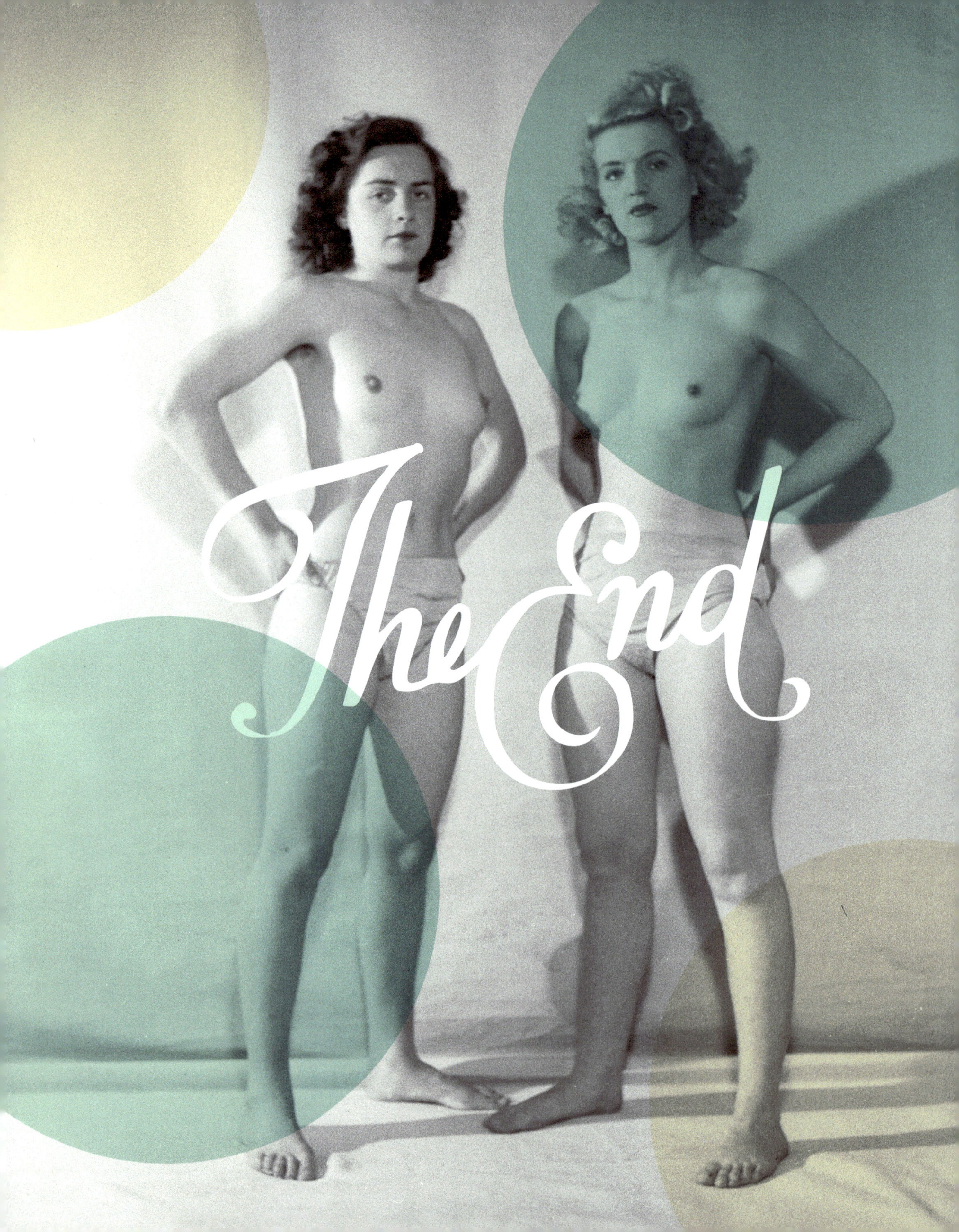
The End

www.ingramcontent.com/pod-product-compliance
Ingram Content Group UK Ltd.
Pitfield, Milton Keynes, MK11 3LW, UK
UKHW061034310726
14089UKWH00010B/237
9781999744113